INTRODUCTION

THE 5 PRIMARY COMPONENTS OF THE MINDSET OF A SUCCESSFUL SEDUCER

I. BE RUTHLESS

Life is a short, and then you die.

Your life is composed of a certain amount of TIME TOKENS (a series of moments) and when these TIME TOKENS are gone, then you cease to exist on earth.

Your days are numbered, bitch.

You have a limited amount of this INCREDIBLY VALU-ABLE RESOURCE, so it's essential that you don't give out your TIME TOKENS for free and without much thought. **Be highly selective** about who you give these TIME TOKENS to. **If a woman is taking up your hours, then she better be fucking worth it.**[1]

Here in New York City, a dentist will charge $120 for just a 10 minute consultation. It doesn't matter how much pain you're in, the dentist doesn't have a "savior complex" and won't give away his time to your for free because of your entitlement. The Dentist will tell freeloaders to "FUCK OFF" because his business is not a charity. Even if the Dentist doesn't say "I don't give a fuck about your problems if I'm not being paid" **it will be implied with his actions** - e.g. not being available to freeloaders, and having lots of excuses as to why he simply "can't" be available to you (See Law #53: Action Reveals All).

Some men waste years of their life running a Time and Psychological Energy Charity for low quality unworthy women - instead of running a ruthlessly efficient clear GAME PLAN for GETTING SEX.[2]

- **Be clear about what you want out** of the sexual marketplace to make the most out of your finite time.
- **Be clear about what you <u>don't</u> want,** so you can assertively communicate clear boundaries, and have the ability to say "no".

Be highly selective about those who you allow within your inner-circle.

Learn this right now and right here: **if a low quality woman is taking up a lot of your time (without giving a substantial amount of value in return), dump her and never look back. Period. Bottom line.**

Having the ability to walk away from connections don't serve you: is a fundamentally crucial aspect of manhood. Simply knowing that you have the ability to walk away: will give you a sense of real confidence, and will come across in your interactions with women - giving you a competitive sexy edge.

WOMANESE 101 (UPDATED: JUNE 27, 2023)

HOW TO TALK AND FLIRT WITH WOMEN, MAKE GIRLS ADDICTED TO BEING WITH YOU

SECRETS OF THE PICKUP ARTIST
BOOK 2

CORY SMITH, AUTHOR OF @PUA_DATING_TIPS

You are constantly sending signals out to women - consciously and unconsciously. Some signals are seductive and lead to sex occurring (such as signals that convey that you are THE PRIZE, THE SELECTOR, and A HIGH STATUS AMAZING CATCH). Other signals are anti-seductive (such as putting up with bullshit, weak body-language, being overly available, making her your Life Purpose etc).

What you believe about yourself (you hold yourself in high esteem; you have the belief that "ANY WOMAN IN MY INNER-CIRCLE IS FORTUNATE TO HAVE ME; I AM A WOMAN'S BEST OPTION") **and what you believe about what you have to offer women** (your competitive value proposition in the sexual marketplace) **is intuitively sensed by women.**

This bears repeating: what you believe about yourself and what you have to offer women will intuitively

be sensed by women. A <u>high status self-image</u> leads to sexy <u>high status behaviors.</u>

- For instance: women intuitively know that that an ELITE HIGH STATUS MAN (a man who is in the top 1% of society) has REAL OPTIONS with other women and has HIGH STANDARDS. Hence, she intuitively senses that he won't put up with bullshit (low quality behaviors) for too long; there will come a point when he will just be fed up and walk away. **If a man allows himself to be treated like a doormat, then women will start to view him as having the same worth as a doormat.**[3]
- **In contrast, if you believe you're gold then this will come across in how you conduct yourself and be intuitively sensed by those around you.**
- If you believed you were GOLD and what you have to offer is GOLD, then you wouldn't stay in a situation where other people were treating you like shit, because you would know that it would be easy for you find new relationships with new people (after all, you are offering GOLD). You would naturally have higher standards, and convey a willingness to walk away - which ironically will make women like you even more.

A key fundamental in learning to speak Womense is to condition your mind that you are GOLD, what you have to offer is metaphorical GOLD, and your time is GOLD; when you truly believe this then you'll unconsciously communicate this through your body-language, actions, and words. For instance: simply feeling powerful leads to exuding powerful body-language.[4] As I explain in a later chapter in this book, behaviors stem from beliefs.

It's also worth noting that **beliefs are contagious.** By changing your beliefs about yourself, you'll change women's beliefs about you.[5]

ASK YOURSELF THESE 6 QUESTIONS TO GIVE YOURSELF A REALITY CHECK:

- #1) How much is your time really worth?
- #2) **Put a price-tag on your time** to gain a better perspective. If a magical potion would take away a year of your life in exchange for $10,000 would you agree? If someone paid you an hourly rate to stare at a wall and do nothing; what would your price be?
- #3) Your time is worth a fucking lot, so why do you give it away like it's cheap by being overly available to anyone who asks? **Why do you feel inclined to say "yes" to things when you really want to say "no, I am busy"?**
- #4) Why do you waste psychological energy on things/people that are unworthy of you? Why do you allow yourself to be swept up into a woman's bullshit drama over petty issues - instead of focusing on your own personal development and goals?
- #5) You are a biological ticking time bomb headed towards an irreversible end. Do you make every day count? Do you use every hour of the day? Do you use every minute of every hour?
- #6) The Corona Virus Pandemic has made it ultra clear that life is fragile. Do you live with the awareness that one day the life force within you will be gone? If so, what do you want to accomplish before the Final End? **Make a Final Bucket list**

titled "Things that I want to GET DONE Before I
Go Away Forever."

THE WOMENESE PARADOX

While it is true that this entire book is dedicated to understanding the secret language of women: Womenese, it is also
true that you don't want to waste away your valuable time
getting caught up in a woman's silly bullshit and pointless
drama (created because she is starving for attention).

THE 7th QUESTION

Every minute you spend obsessing over "What did she really
mean when she said X" could have been a minute that you
spent investing in yourself, executing daily goals, or meeting
new girls. **While you're thinking about her, do you think she
is thinking about you?**

THE KEY TO SOLVING THE PARADOX

Always focus on the primary goal of understanding and
speaking Womenese; <u>the primary goal is to efficiently and
effectively have sex with a beautiful woman</u> - which leads to
a long term mutually beneficial sexual relationship that
includes countless additional nights of sex.** You want to
accomplish this primary goal with Bullshit Encountered
Counter at null (or as close to null as possible), and not getting
sucked into time-wasting drama.

   <u>The secondary goal is to develop GAME SKILLS, so that
you can go out, meet and seduce a new woman - if the neces-
sity arrives.</u> Don't wait for a breakup to start developing GAME
SKILLS. Develop GAME SKILLS SHARP and KEEP THEM
SHARP - even if you currently are in a relationship right

now.[6]In the event of the relationship ending, you want to still have the essential skills necessary to meet women and generate the value that women feed on, ON-THE-READY.

It's important to keep this always keep the primary and secondary goals in mind at all times when dealing with women, so you don't lose the forest for the trees and you don't waste psychological energy on a lot of the stupid petty bullshit that women talk about. You want to enter The Womanverse so you can get practical knowledge that leads you to FUCK HER IN THE PUSSY - not so you can get lost in an endless blackhole of abstract theory.

I will be guide on this educational journey and hit you with various game-changing epiphanies. Let's get started with this introduction by talking:

- about common traps in the sexual marketplace,
- the overall mindset that you should have when dealing with women,
- the goals of speaking Womenese,
- the cardinal rules of seduction,
- how to be a badass Alpha Who FUCKS, and
- how to communicate the sexy irresistible trait of confidence.

FIVE COMMON SEXUAL MARKETPLACE TRAPS THAT MEN FALL INTO

- **#1) THE FRIEND ZONE TRAP** Think about how guys are stuck in one-sided friend-zone "relationships" with women that are not sexually receptive. The solution is: MAKE A MOVE. Making

<u>a move will force a woman to either get involved with you on a sexual level, or fuck off.</u> A key concept in speaking Womenese is to understand that a woman's actions reveal more about her than her words. Thus, it's prudent to force a woman into making a behavioral choice, so that you can make an accurate assessment of the situation.

- **#2) THE TOXIC RELATIONSHIP TRAP** Think about guys stuck in dead-end toxic relationships where they are treated like shit, and stepped over like they're doormats. They treat the woman like a goddess, while allowing themselves to be treated like trash. They've idealized this woman in their mind, developed feelings for her, and rationalize her bad behavior as "love doesn't come easy; it must be earned". Don't let a woman treat you like shit; <u>have enough self-respect to walk away from a woman who isn't pulling her weight in a "relationship".</u> When you know you have GAME SKILLS, you won't be afraid to walk away because a better higher-quality woman is right around the corner.

- **#3) THE ENDLESS DATES TO NOWHERE TRAP** Think about guys spending months fantasizing about a woman who they're too pussy to make a move on. She might not even be aware of their existence. In the process of waiting for months, they lose their own self-esteem and confidence level. <u>If a woman makes you wait for months, in the vast *vast* majority of cases: her pussy isn't worth the wait.</u> Opportunity Cost is the price of lost opportunities. You are so obsessed with one particular pussy, you didn't even notice the dozens of other pussies that were available. Don't have endless dates to nowhere, or be the perpetual texting penpal. You have to be constantly making reasonable progress (at a reasonable pace) towards sex, or she needs to fuck off.

- **#4) THE OBSESSION TRAP** Think about guys obsessed over one particular woman. They'll spend all of their time, and mental energy thinking about her constantly. <u>They're so busy obsessing over one particular woman, they'll stop developing their sexual market-value, miss out on opportunities with other women, and even lose valuable male friendships with cool guys.</u> You might find a relatively high quality woman to be in a relationship with, but this doesn't mean that you should stop developing yourself, stop focusing on your Life Mission, start losing your competitive edge in the sexual marketplace, and start losing valued male friendships.

- **#5) THE LOW QUALITY WOMAN TRAP** Think about how much of a person's life and psychological health is wasted by spending time with low quality women who infect his mind with negative emotions and petty energy-draining drama. If you are a high status man, you shouldn't need to settle down with a woman who has severe issues; aim higher. Your psychological resources are finite, so if a woman is taking them then she better be fucking worth it. Focus on high quality women; cut out low quality women.

Falling into one of these traps is months (sometimes years) of valuable TIME TOKENS being poured down the toilet. Spending time on a woman who is a good sexual potential is like watering a seed that turns into a plant that bears fruits, but spending time on:

- a toxic woman (with severe emotional baggage),
- on a woman who has friend zoned,
- on a woman who has low interest (and unavailable for in-person meetups),
- on a woman who is perpetually in a bad mood and always finds things to complain about,
- on a woman who has perpetual problems that she needs saving from because she is incredibly incompetent,

you is like watering a rock. Pouring more water is not going to magically change the rock into a plant; if you keep doing what you're doing then you'll keep getting what you're getting. You have to kick the rock to the curb, go find time-worthy seeds and **never look back**. Next level behaviors lead to next level results.

In the case of a toxic woman who is a relationship dead-end, it's better to move on with your life, **because no pussy is worth your peace of mind.** Even if you fuck her, the psychological toll is not worth it, because that's psychological energy that you could have spent developing better leads that are of healthier connections.

No pussy is worth your self-respect, and sexual market-value. Even if you fuck her in the end, think about how you've lost opportunities with other girls in the process.

I'm about to say something that is incredibly politically incorrect (and should not be shared with blue-pilled male associates): **women have different levels of quality in sexual relationships.** Not every woman that you can fuck is worth fucking. Some low quality garbage should be left in the garbage.

In contrast, there are higher quality women out there that are worth getting into a long-term sexual relationship with.

THE GOALS OF SPEAKING, SIGNALING, UNDERSTANDING, AND OBSERVING THE SECRET LANGUAGE KNOWN AS WOMENESE.

When you meet a beautiful woman who is worthy of your time, you want to be fluent in Womenese to be able to:

- Truly understand her thoughts, feelings, and actions, so that you can behave in a manner that resonates positively. **Do more of what is seductively impactful, and less of what is seductively repulsive.**
- Understand what she means when she says specific things, so that you can calibrate your strategy accordingly. A key principle of this book is: **a woman's words reveal the mechanism of her psych.**
- Understand the signals that she is sending out with her body language and what they mean, so you can capitalize on "DOWN TO FUCK RIGHT NOW" signals. **If you miss the DTF Signals, you won't fuck her at the moment that she is sexually available.** Be aware of the signals that a woman unconsciously (or consciously) sends out when she wants to fuck, so that you'll be able to notice them when they occur in real time, and you'll act on them. When opportunity meets a man who is ready, sex happens.
- Understand the truth behind the male-to-female dynamic, so that you can leverage the variables in this dynamic to your seductive advantage. A woman wants you to play the dominant masculine role in the relationship, so she can play the submissive feminine role. **Treat a woman like a woman, so she**

<u>can feel sexy.</u> Submission within a woman unleashes her sexual side.

- Understand what you have to do specifically to solidify a physical connection. <u>It is your responsibility as a man to physically escalate the interaction towards sex because a woman's ego prevents her from doing this that will make her feel slutty.</u>

Womenese boils down to these 6 mediums that give off signals:

- **#1) Thoughts**
- **#2) Feelings**
- **#3) Words**
- **#4) Actions**
- **#5) Body Language**
- **#6) Social Media**

The first 5 factors tend to feed off each other. For instance: thoughts lead to feelings lead to words lead to actions and vice versa.

The 6th factor is a woman's social media lifestyle which are quite revealing about her and sometimes can reveal what her thoughts are about you.

INDICATORS TO GAUGE A WOMAN'S QUALITY, SO YOU DON'T WASTE YOUR TIME LOOKING THROUGH METAPHORICAL GARBAGE.

A HIGHER-QUALITY WOMAN WILL:

- #1) **inspire you to be your best** (doesn't bring out your worst),
- #2) **bring value to your life** (your life is better with her than without her in it),
- #3) **is frugal when making decisions that impact your wallet** (is conscious about your wellbeing when making decisions that could impact you),
- #4) **respect you** - fostering confidence levels/building your self-image (a woman's respect is essential for sexual attraction to stay high), and
- #5) **create a positive vibe** (creating a feel-good environment that is conducive to your personal development).

IN CONTRAST, A LOWER-QUALITY WOMAN WILL:

- #6) **constantly complain** (something is always "wrong"),
- #7) **criticize** (it seems to be her life mission to find out what is missing within who you are, instead of being grateful for your strengths),
- #8) **seems to always be in a bad mood** (a key aspect in learning to speak Womenese is being able to identify the emotional states of others and the variables that influence these emotional states),
- #9) **create drama/chaos** - making it more difficult for you to be successful in your life purpose (because the drama takes up a lot of your time and psychological resources),
- #10) **only cares about what she can get out of you and what you stand for** (rather than your personality and who you actually are),

- **#11) isn't kind to strangers** (because she is obsessed with her own self-gain and can't see past her own sense of self-centeredness),
- **#12) tends to talk negatively about other people** (including her past relationships and the people that are presently in her life), and
- **#13) post semi-clad IG photos** because she's consciously (or unconsciously) fishing for other guys.

Some female characteristics are more important to some men than than others because preferences are subjective. As I discussed in "The Sexcalation System" *(2nd Edition)* it's important for you to know what you want out of the Sexual Marketplace through the exercise of:

- "Precise Visualization",
- verbalizing your goals/visualizing your vision every morning, and
- writing down what you want.

<u>The most important indicator of a high quality woman is sexual availability towards you.</u> Sex is an incredibly important aspect of a relationship for both partners involved. No, that is not being petty; it's being hyper realistic and practical. **A woman becomes emotionally invested to the man that she has sex with and is physically intimate with** - unless she is a prostitute and has learned to detach herself.[7]

Likewise, <u>a man values a woman and is inspired to invest into the relationship when he is fucking her (with orgasams included).</u> This is why sex occurring is essential for the health of the relationship for both partners.[8]

THE CARDINAL RULE OF SEDUCTION #1: FUCK ME, OR FUCK OFF.

In the case of a woman who has friend-zoned you, you have to start making moves that will lead to sex occurring - adopting the mindsets of:

- "blow me, or blow me out"
- "fuck me, or fuck off", and
- "FUCK or BOUNCE."

By being overtly sexual, you're forcing a woman to make a choice - (option 1) either fall into your frame, or (option 2) walk away.

REGARDLESS OF HER CHOICE: YOU WIN.

- **OPTION 1:** if she falls into your frame by allowing you to make sexual advances, then you'll eventually have sex with her.
- **OPTION 2:** if she walks away, then you stop wasting time and psychological energy on a sexual dead-end.

Express sexual intent. If she responds on a sexual level then good (*you got what you wanted*). If she rejects you then that's also good (*because now she'll stop wasting your time and you can focus on better leads*). By making sexual advances, you can't lose regardless of the outcome, so there is no reason to be anxious over sexual escalation.

THE NICE GUY DELUSION

- **The nice guy will rationalize spending hours upon hours with a woman who is not sexually available** by giving into her frame of entitlement, and being mislead by his Savior Complex.
- He was brought up to be a "gentleman" and mistakenly assumes that being a "gentleman" always being available to **help women (without getting value in return) because it's "the right thing to do"** - **regardless of how psychological energy or personal time it costs him.**

His actions of wasting time and putting up with bullshit communicate volumes (to women who notice these subtle signals) about his worth. It communicates that he doesn't value his time, and thus women don't really value him. The moment they get all of the value that they can from him, they're gone. After all, the entire relationship was based on a one sided platonic providership.

The nice guy should learn three things immediately:

- **(1) he doesn't owe women anything,**
- **(2) a woman has to be sexually available for her to even warrant his time** (or at least allow for physical escalation to occur at a reasonable pace, so that it eventually does lead to sex within a reasonable time frame)[9], and
- **(3) to be worthy of a relationship, the woman has to reciprocate by providing substantial value of her own** (other than just having a hole in between her legs; remember: women only value what they work for).

THE CARDINAL RULE OF SEDUCTION #2: WHEN IT COMES TO SEX, PAY MORE ATTENTION TO WHAT SHE DOES THAN WHAT SHE SAYS.

This is a book about understanding the Womenese language. Understand this right now and right here: women speak the loudest with their actions. You've heard the phrase "A picture is worth a thousand words." **<u>A single action reveals more about a woman than 10,000 words.</u>** A woman could verbally bullshit you from morning to night, but her actions and body-language reveal the truth about the situation.

IF SHE:

- allows physical escalation to occur on an intimate level,
- initiates touching by herself,
- qualifies herself to you (e.g. gives you reasons why you should be with her by explaining different ways that she is awesome),
- moves with you to an isolated spot,
- brings up the subject of sex by herself, or
- initiates interactions first AND makes time to see you on one-on-one dates:

then she is into you, and there is sexual potential. This is true even if she is verbally dismissive and says "the wrong things". I repeat: this is true even if on the surface the words that she uses seem to portray you in a negative light. **When actions differ from words, trust the former.**

Words convey what a woman wants to be. Actions convey who she is now. The smart seducer behaves according to how women are - not how they wish to be. He pays attention to their actions and body-language to ascertain the truth. <u>Much of Womenese is unspoken</u>.

THE CARDINAL RULE OF SEDUCTION #3: ALWAYS RETAIN YOUR LEVERAGE.

Be acutely aware of the value that you are giving her that she needs, and values. Retain that leverage.

THE CARDINAL RULE OF SEDUCTION #4: ALWAYS RETAIN WALK-AWAY POWER.

Time is life itself. To give it out to a woman, she must be WORTHY. If she isn't worthy or proves to be unworthy later on in the relationship, then walk away. <u>Always always always retain leverage and the ability to walk away.</u> Women are like children, and need to be dealt with by having a firm hand.

Women have the irrational emotions of a child. This inner-child is always within her but masked because she has learned to appear adultish for the sake of her professional life. Smart seducers know to look past the fake facade of her appearing like a mature adult, and communicate to the inner-child that is within her; this style of communication is known as flirting. One key concept of flirting is to be high status, and a high status man's power is in his ability to walk way because he has other options and the game skills to generate more options.

<u>You have to be ruthless in cutting out women who are wasting your fucking time.</u> Be merciless when rejecting

women who are unworthy. I assure you that a woman is incredibly ruthless when it comes to rejecting men that she sees to be of low worth, so why should you be different? Don't give women an advantage they wouldn't give you.

A master seducer is efficient. When he meets a woman, he thinks her through a live funnel. This funnel involves constantly leading the interaction towards sex. Life is too short to play indirect game that spans months. You have to consistently be moving the connection towards physical intimacy by doing a series of moves. If you spend 5 time tokens achieving something that should have only taken 1 time token then you're just inefficient; don't spend 5 dates to fuck her if you could have fucked her on the first day.

SPEAK WITH YOUR ACTIONS

Women are in abundance - with more turning 18 years of age every minute - but your time is not. Treat your time with respect because time is life itself. [10]

If you don't even respect your time, women won't either. A key concept in speaking Womenese is that you are communicating to women through your actions. YOUR ACTIONS SEND A MESSAGE. By not always being available, you are training the woman to value your time in a language that she truly understands: consequences.

OPERANT CONDITIONING; HOW TO CONDITION A WOMAN TO DO WHAT YOU WANT

Women are like cute puppies. **Attention is the currency.** They are being trained by how you consciously or unconsciously reward them with attention and expressions of emotions.

- **RULE #1:** Female behavior (whether it's good, or bad behavior) that you reward with <u>attention</u> will be repeated.
- **RULE #2:** Female behavior (whether it's good, or bad behavior) that you reward with an **emotional reaction** will be repeated.
- **RULE #3:** Female behavior that is completely ignored and that you are "emotionally numb to" will subside. Hence, <u>withdrawing attention and emotions</u> is an effective strategy for punishing bad behavior, to ensure that the bad behavior does not repeat itself.

.A key concept in speaking Womenese is to understand that Women should be trained like an animal master trains adorable, cuddly puppies - with a firm hand and being careful to <u>give much more attention for positive behavior than negative behavior.</u>

Within her is a child that never matured. This inner-child craves attention. Communicate directly to this child by giving attention (and emotionally expressions) when she does what you want, and withdrawing attention (and emotional expressions) when she doesn't. Remember: attention, fun, and ego validation are forms of value that plays as the currency of the night.

<u>Create the conditions for it be more fun and emotionally enticing for a woman to go along the seduction process than for her to against it.</u> Women just do what feels good and uplifts their spirits, while avoiding that which feels bad and dampens their spirits. Being with you and doing what you want, should be a clear emotional win.

- **Practical example of operatnt conditioning in action:** In the context of physical escalation, the moment a woman doesn't allow for an advancement of physical escalation to occur should be the moment that you temporarily withdraw attention, emotion, fun, and the value that you have been providing her. This way she'll miss what she used to have, and realize that it's more fun to just comply with what you want.

$\sim$

II. BE THE PREDATOR.

Don't wait to be saved. No one is coming to save you.[11] You have to be your own savior. It is your duty to be a fighter for yourself - just like you would be a fighter for your best friend. **Be your own best friend and take care of yourself.**

You see, everyone is too busy obsessing over themselves to prioritize you. You have only yourself to rely upon. If you don't fight for yourself then you will be lost. It's imperative that you PUT YOURSELF FIRST, take value, and ensure that your goals are met. **Just like a woman looks out for herself - you must look out for your own interests.**[12]

As mentioned a moment ago, a key concept in speaking Womense is sending a message with your actions. You can lecture a woman for 10 minutes straight, or you can say nothing and communicate all of that in a single 5 second action. By being a man who is on his mission in life and takes action to achieve his daily goals, you are non-verbally communicating to women that you value yourself. <u>Women value men that value themselves because they are biologically designed to feed off a guy's vibe, self-image, and perspective.</u>

Even in a relationship, continue to run attraction-generating game and develop your sexual market-value. Game is as relevant in a ten year relationship as it is relevant when you first meet a woman. This is why there is no such thing as retiring from game; you are always playing the game - whether you realize it or not. <u>The game never sleeps. Hence, it's essential that you increase your sexual market value on a consistent basis (over a long period of time) to be head and shoulders above the competition.</u>

Don't you get it? A woman is constantly on the lookout to trade up. She can't help but follow her hypergamous nature and crave to capture the highest value man that she can. **A woman will always go for the best option available to her.** In the digital age, women have greater ability to have access to top-tier men because of apps like IG, Snapchat and TikTok. Hence, it's imperative that YOU BE THE HIGHEST VALUE MAN. By being at the APEX, even if she decides to act upon her inner-instincts to trade up: there is no one else to trade up to because you are "the most up" option. BE THE CREME DE LA CREME.

Improve yourself by at least 1% every single day. Even marginal consistent improvements ADD UP FAST, and over the aggregate add up to something very substantial. **Self-development is a long-term game.** One does not transform into a Casanova overnight, but rather its a process of conscious self-improvement that spans years. Power does not randomly fall upon a man, but it is SEIZED. Excellence of character is forged.

Power is a game and if you're not at the field being a player - you're usually the one who is being played by an actual player. In life there are two types of people:

- **TYPE #1:** A Wolf (🐺 Predator), and
- **TYPE #2:** A Sheep (🐑 Prey).

The wolf use the sheep for their own personal gain - just like employers use employees for their own personal gain, or how Alpha Males tool Beta Males. **In the game of life, strong** men control the weak, but the clever and skilled control the strong. If you are not part of the predator crowd then you're by default part of the prey crowd. **In life, you have to be a predator. <u>You have to be extremely aggressive in going after what you want.</u>**

III. BE AN APEX ALPHA.

ALPHA TRAITS

- One of the defining traits of the Alpha Male is that he TAKES WHAT HE WANTS. **While the beta male is drowning in "What ifs" and perpetual analysis, <u>the Alpha Male TAKES ACTION TO GET WHAT HE WANTS.</u>**
- **The Alpha Male cultivates the proactive behavioral tendencies of taking consistent, daily, focused, MASSIVE action to bring himself closer to his goals.**
- **The Alpha Male values himself and his own personal agenda more than anything else in the world.** That is why he is able to advance forward in life at incredible speeds - leaving people-pleasing suck-ups in the dust. While soy boys are wasting their valuable life force slaving away to please a pussy they've pedestalized, the Alpha Male is busy GETTING SHIT DONE and CLIMBING THE PATH TO POWER IN SOCIETY.

BETA TRAITS

- The Beta Males cultivates passivity tendencies. The Beta male waits for sexual opportunities to find him, while the Alpha male creates them.
- The Beta Male is stuck in a perpetual procrastination trap that spans years (and sometimes his entire pathetic existence).
- The Beta is constantly "getting ready to take radical action" but never actually hits the "take radical action NOW" phase. He is "too smart for his own good" - stuck in never-ending overthinking.

THE ALPHA VERSUS BETA SPECTRUM:

Whether your skin is thick or thin determines your success with women. The Beta male doesn't act upon on sexual opportunities because he is terrified of rejection (his fragile ego can't handle the burn), but the Alpha Male acts upon sexual opportunities immediately because he knows that occasional rejection is part of the game; **the Alpha Male doesn't give a fuck if a woman rejects him because he knows that he can get another.** He who fears rejection has already granted women too much power over him; he who retains "Walk Away Power" saves himself from misery and being dragged into toxic and one-sided relationships.

Always retain Walk Away Power and that's done by having other options in your life, having sharp game (so you know that you can go out on any day and get a woman), and continuously raising your sexual market value and sharpening your skills. MAKE EVERY DAY COUNT.

The Beta Male is plagued with self-doubt, but the Alpha Male makes decisions with confidence and decisiveness -

making him a natural leader. <u>How you behave in life, is how you behave with women.</u> If you find yourself constantly doubting yourself then this kind of behavioral tendencies will be relevant when dealing with women as well. This is why it is important that you DOMINATE EVERYTHING.

HOLD NOTHING BACK. YOU ARE THE CHAOS. YOU ATTACK LIFE WITH FULL FORCE, AND GET SHIT HANDLED. NO MATTER WHAT LIFE THROWS AT YOU, YOU FUCKING HANDLE IT.

<u>Being an Alpha Male communicates volumes to women simply by the way that you live your life, and the values you stand for.</u> Being an Alpha Male makes women WANT to follow your lead - creating a river trickling down their panties. Remember: **a worthy Dom creates a willing Submissive.**

IV. YOU BECOME WHAT YOU THINK, SO THINK POSITIVE.

8 MORE COMMON TRAPS IN THE SEXUAL MARKETPLACE

- #6) **THE TIME SINKS TRAP** spending countless hours binge watching TV shows instead of **developing and sharpening high demand skills**,
- #7) **THE SMALL POND TRAP** Wasting incredibly valuable time hanging out with loser friends instead of **cultivating a tribe of HIGHLY DRIVEN KILLERS**,
- #8) **LIVING IN THE PAST TRAP** Engaging in emotional suicide by endlessly thinking about prior rejections, past mistakes and futile pointless

thinking ("what if I would have done ___?" or "If only I would have avoided ___") instead of <u>having a VISION, creating GOALS for that VISION, TAKING ACTION DAILY, and EXECUTING LIKE THE TERMINATOR,</u>

- **#9) BEING A PEOPLE-PLEASER TRAP** Being obsessed over low-quality women who don't care about them in, who treat them like shit and don't have much to offer besides a used-pussy instead of focusing on further <u>developing yourself to BECOME AN APEX PREDATOR.</u> When you're focusing on other people (by endlessly scrolling through their social media feed) then you aren't focusing on yourself. <u>Self-development requires a significant level of selfishness because it takes a ton of fucking time, and energy;</u> if you're busy running favors for other people then you won't have leftover time/energy for yourself for your own development.

- **#10) THE NEGATIVE MIND TRAP** Constantly repeating negative thoughts such as "the situation is hopeless", "I am so disgusting that no women will want me", or "learning self-help theories is useless because it never leads to anywhere" instead of focusing on your strengths, talents and creating a <u>HIGHLY PRACTICAL PLAN OF SPECIFIC BEHAVIORS THAT LEAD TO RESULTS.</u>

Why do guys FUCK THEMSELVES UP by engaging in self-sabotage behavior?

#11) TAKING THE BRIBE OF THE DARK SIDE TRAP
Don't you get it motherfucker? **There is a certain kind of**

addiction to misery. Guys engage in self-sabotage behavior because there is a hidden emotional-pay off.

- By saying things like "I am worthless. No women will want me - no matter how hard I try" you are able to create justification for being lazy.
- By thinking self-sabotage negative thoughts such as "There is no point in approaching beautiful women because I know that it won't work anyways" then you release the responsibility off your shoulders, and you get to waste away valuable evenings playing video-games without feeling guilty.
- By focusing on past mistakes you can procrastinate and avoid confronting challenges in the present.

If you look closely there is always some hidden benefit to engaging in a self-sabotage behavior that is FUCKING YOU UP. If you can identify the hidden payoff then you can bribe yourself by counteracting it. Create a bigger incentive for doing what's right and living a life that leads to COMPLETELY DOMINATING EVERYTHING THAT YOU DO.

SEDUCTION IS A LIFESTYLE.

#12: "THE PLEASURE HABITS DIE HARD" TRAP

You'll know where you will be in 5 years based on your current rate of daily progress. You have to kill bad negative habits (that are addictive because they provide a sort of pleasure) by replacing them with *positive habit*s that you have personally engineered to give a greater amount of pleasure than the *negative habits*. **A successful seducer has a set of lifestyle habits that lead to him meeting and having sex with beautiful women - almost on autopilot. Hence, seduction is a lifestyle - living these daily habits day in and day out.**

The Stacker Method for Getting Laid

- For instance: create a <u>daily habit</u> of getting work done or hanging out in areas where there is a <u>high traffic of beautiful women who are receptive to meeting strangers</u>. These places include but are not limited to coffee shops, the library, Yoga club, a local park, or various social clubs at your local college campus. Then set a personal goal to talk to at least one girl at this location every single day. Don't be a lazy ass motherfucking bitch ass motherfucker cunt soy boy bastard who is afraid to leave the house; if that's you then close this book right now and live under the bed at your mama's house (still suckling her warm milk). **This book isn't for BIIIIATCHE PUSSIES.**

- Another example: create a <u>daily habit</u> of following up on the leads that you have acquired. This is simple as having a set time each day (perhaps 10:00-10:30pm) where you call up the girls on your phone to flirt, and sustain the connection.

- Finally, have a weekly habit of inviting women out for cool events in the city during the weekend.

<u>**First you create your lifestyle habits and then these lifestyle habits create you.**</u> The problem is that some guys have lifestyle habits that are destroying them (sleeping in late, hanging out with the wrong crowd of people, being in a micro environment that is toxic, being addicted to fapping etc) and they are having difficulty overcoming these behavioral tendencies because the behaviors happen automatically - on autopilot - without their conscious awareness. The goal is to consciously create a set of positive habits that replace the negative ones and

then stack positive habits until you **BECOME A FORCE TO BE RECKONED WITH.**

V. EXUDE EXTREME CONFIDENCE. YOU ARE THE GREAT PRIZE TO BE WON.

#13: The Being Afraid-to-Make-a-Move Trap

MAKING MOVES ON A WOMAN AND GETTING REJECTED IS INFINITELY BETTER than not making moves on a woman and not getting rejected. In Pook's words "Rejection is better than regret."

Every time you advance (do something specific on a particular woman in order to lead the interaction to sex), you learn something in the process. This is true - even if you are met with a harsh blowout. He who keeps advancing will eventually learn enough to be a master.

In contrast, someone who has a fragile ego won't escalate (and won't even try) because he is too terrified of getting blown-out: will learn NOTHING. Someone who doesn't even attempt to make moves on women sends a signal to his unconscious mind that he is UNWORTHY. He rejected himself because he allowed his limiting beliefs of his self-worth win over.

OLD BELIEF:

- *"I am too unattractive for any woman to like me, so I won't even try because it won't work anyways."*
- *"I don't want to approach because it will be cringe, and I'll feel like shit."*

REFRAME:

- *"I have a lot to offer women. Being with me is one of THE BEST CHOICES SHE CAN MAKE."*
- *"Regardless of the output of this particular approach, I am going to have fun and learn something from it. Even the worst rejections, make the best stories."*

Be acutely aware of your strengths and talents. Write them down. By being aware of what you're good at then you have it ready-at-hand to be used to help you in life. Women find excellence in almost any particular field to be incredibly attractive. Know what you're exceptional in, and then go to venues that where people gather (women included) who value that which you're exceptional in. A key in speaking Womenese is to show the best parts of yourself.

MY DEAR SON, I ASK OF YOU ONLY ONE THING THAT YOU SHOULD REMEMBER. REMEMBER THAT: <u>HE WHO HESITATES IS LOST.</u>

Why is confidence the ultimate sex appeal?

Just like you are attracted to slim women (because slimness is an indicator of fertility), women are attracted to CONFIDENCE (because confidence is a solid indicator of competence). Generally speaking: confident men are KILLING IT IN LIFE which is why they are confident in the first place.

Women don't have the time to give each guy a FULL CHANCE and to LEARN EVERYTHING ABOUT HIM, so they use shortcuts such as looking at a man's level of confidence, style, and his status within society, to ascertain if he is worth getting to know. These shortcuts save them a lot of time.[13]

Confidence and status will get you in the door; conversation, escalation and giving value will get you into the bedroom.

4 ESSENTIAL KEYS TO HAVING CONFIDENCE AND HOW TO CONVEY IT IN A MANNER THAT TURNS WOMEN ON

- 1// Be extremely confident when you are around women. Don't just be a little confident around women; be <u>extremely</u> confident.
- 2// **It is better to be irrationally confident than rationally insecure.** Even if you have plenty of reasons to be insecure, focus on the reasons why you are THE BOSS. Show confidence - even if "it doesn't make sense". **Be extremely confident - <u>even if it's on an irrational level.</u>**
- 3// If you aren't feeling confident, take some time to **verbalize your strengths**, talents, skills and the type of value that you have to offer women. Meditate on your strong points, and leverage them in interactions with women. **<u>If you aren't using what you're really good at then you missed the fucking point, bitch motherfucker.</u>**
- 4// **Stand up for yourself.** Spend time with people that bring you up, and inspire you to be your best. Don't spend time with people that put you down - compromising your self-esteem in the process. Have standards, boundaries, and a healthy sense of independence. Further, don't ascertain your level of worth based on your results with women, or the opinion of other people.

Just like confidence is sexy, self-doubt is repulsive to women. Hesitation is a show of self-doubt. Hesitation comes from being unsure of yourself, and delaying taking action, so that you can confirm your own worth in your mind. Even if you have legitimate questions about yourself and what you are doing, when you are in the field **EXUDE 100% STRENGTH AND A BULLETPROOF FRAME.**

Make decisions with certainty and decisiveness. Women will follow a leader who believes in his path. **BE A WARRIOR ON HIS LIFE PURPOSE.**

SEND A MESSAGE WITH YOUR ACTIONS, WHAT YOU STAND FOR, AND THE WAY THAT YOU LIVE YOUR LIFE

Simply by the way that you live your life, you are sending signals to women about your worth (or lack of it). Understand this right now and right here: **most of Womenese is non-verbal.** This is why guys often fuck themselves up by sending low-worth signals to women without even being aware that they are sending out these signals.

By living the life of an Alpha Warrior who

- knows what he wants out of life,
- has clearly defined goals that are reviewed daily,
- goes after what he wants aggressively,
- values his time,
- respects himself enough to retain Walk Away Power,
- lives in accordance with his values,
- doesn't waste time with petty drama,
- doesn't put but with second class behavior,
- doesn't dwell around negative unambitious people, and
- doesn't waste time going on endless conversations and dates to nowhere .

you'll unconsciously send "I AM SEXY" signals to women.

1. Every woman has a vagina. Some women have something of more substantial value to offer. You have to have an acute understanding what you bring to the table in a relationship because that is going to be a source of tremendous confidence. Then look at what the particular woman you are with is bringing to the table. A relationship is simply a constant value-exchange over a long period of time. If you're doing all of the giving and none of the taking then that is a serious problem. First of all, by not taking any value from the woman who you are dealing with: you won't be that motivated to keep going and keep investing in her. Second of all, a woman is biologically designed to only value what she works for. If she isn't working on your behalf and sweating to jump through hoops to win you over, then she won't really appreciate you. A woman needs to put in effort for you in order to value you. This is why it is not petty to ask "What is doing for me?" and "What does she have to offer besides a used-vagina that guys have used within 24 hours of meeting her?" but rather these questions are practical in nature. Create a pathway for a woman to sweat for you, and she'll appreciate you a thousandfold. In contrast, play easy to get and easy to keep and she'll take you for granted. In this specific issue, you are the same: you're more likely to value and apply the information presented in this book because you paid for it. It's human nature to cherish investments, but disregard the free/easily acquired. Don't hate women for their dark nature; just play the fucking game and WIN.

2. If you don't even have a plan then you are leaving everything to chance and hope. Hope and chance are not effective strategies. **Some plan is better than no plan.** Not bothering to prepare by having a specific strategy for your sex life is plain stupid.

3. Actions create beliefs just like beliefs create actions. The mind is always listening. If you behave like you are a 10, you will come to believe that you are a 10. If you allow a woman to treat you like shit, she will eventually come to believe that you are shit.

4. You become what you think. Thoughts literally shape your emotions, character and decisions. Everything you see around you was once a thought . By thinking positively about yourself, and holding yourself in high esteem in your mind then you foster sexy confidence. **Attack the behaviors, and not the person.** This is a key concept in learning self-help material. Learning self-help content doesn't mean that you suck with women, or that you are awful. It means that you are good, and want to be great!

5. The unconscious mind is more powerful than the conscious mind. Most of your behaviors are on auto-pilot directed by your unconscious mind.

6. It's pathetic to see a high status man get into a relationship and suddenly lose his own identity in the process of creating rapport. It will go as far as

his losing male friendships, personal goals and compromising his life mission. A sexual relationship is a beautiful thing, but NEVER NEVER NEVER let it be at the cost of your soul. There are more things in life than just pussy. Know what your purpose is in life. Create a vision. Have daily goals that you review every day. Pussy is not the end goal. While you are delving into the world of Womenese, don't get lost in it; just gain enough practical knowledge to be effective in dealing with women, but don't get drowned in abstract theories that are irrelevant or non-actionable.

7. A woman who has had many sexual partners compromises her ability to form close bonds.

8. The smart female seducer will use sex as a way to gain power in the relationship.

9. Sex should occur within approximately seven hours accumulated over the span of 1-3 dates.

10. Time is the currency that life runs on. The older you get the less of it you have. The young are the richest, while the old are the poorest.

11. Even if you read every seduction book ever written, you won't get results until you apply what you've learned in the field. What you get out of this book is determined by the extent that you apply the principles in real world situations, and consciously practice the techniques mentioned.

12. Just like a woman goes out of her way to consume value from the man she is with, it's important for you to be clear about what you want in the relationship and TAKE IT. Having a strong sense of purpose and being decisive about what you want out of life are core Alpha Male Traits that TURN WOMEN ON.

13. Women are often better players of the game than men are. Don't be tricked by a pretty face and a facade of submissive ignorance.

FAST START: HOW TO TALK TO GIRLS, 6 FUNDAMENTALS

BE INTERESTING ✎.

1 **. Add energy, enthusiasm, and passion to your words.**
If you don't even care about what you have to say, then don't expect others to care. In contrast, if you think what you have to say is interesting and you're naturally excited about it, then women will be more inclined to listen to you.

Talk about what is interesting to you, and exciting events that have happened to you. When you discuss your life's passions then you'll naturally be enthusiastic. Women feed on the positive energy that you exude when you talk passionately about your Life's Mission.

This is why having a vision that is more important than her is critical. It has been said: "*The best way to get a woman is not be out to get a woman.*" A woman wants to be a helper to your Life Mission - not the Life Mission itself. She yearns to be a part of your ambitious journey to success. Know your purpose. Know the answer to this question "Where do you see yourself five years from now?"

POWER IS THE ULTIMATE SEX APPEAL .

2. Have powerful body-language when communicating with women. Often how you say something is more important than what you are actually saying; hence, your delivery skills are crucial. **You can have the best pickup lines in the world, but if the delivery is off then the pickup lines won't hit.** If you body-language is weak then women won't take you seriously. Here is a checklist for good body-language when communicating with women. Each one of these is incredibly important.

- #1) Be **LOUD.**
- #2) Have a **DEEP TONALITY.**
- #3) Hold **STRONG EYE-CONTACT.**
- #4) Take your time when talking. Talk slower at times to emphasize key points. **GOOD PACING** is vital.
- #5) Use **PAUSES** to build anticipation.
- #6) **TOUCH** to emphasize key points.
- #7) Use **GESTURES** to emphasize key points.
- #8) **TAKE UP SPACE** when talking to women. Keep your feet apart. Have a Power-Posture.
- #9) **HAVE VARIETY** in your tonality, temp and volume.
- #10) Communicate with NON-VERBAL body-language such as your posture, and practiced **FACIAL EXPRESSIONS.**
- #11) Practice emotional regulation techniques and meditation skills to communicate from a position of having a **RESOURCEFUL EMOTIONAL STATE**, and peace of mind. Being relaxed will help you avoid nervous ticks, facial flinches, or signaling stress.

- ☑ #12) Keep your head up, and chest out. Keep your back straight. Lean back. **OWN THE SPACE.**
- ☑ #12) Feel good. Enjoy the experience in the present moment. Flash a **GENUINE SMILE.**
- ☑ #13) Amplify your volume and **SPEAK CLEARLY.** Articulate yourself well.
- ☑ #14) Sit down, lean against the wall, or get into a comfortable position. This is known as **LOCKING IN.** Confident men don't position themselves in an uncomfortable position when communicating.
- ☑ #15) Command the environment. Move things around. Control and adjust things in the environment. Behave like **THE PLACE YOU ARE IN IS YOUR HOME.**
- ⚫ #16) DON'T ⚫ Talk quietly. Talking quietly is the most effective way to have women ignore you. If you don't even take yourself seriously then why should women?
- ⚫ #17) DON'T ⚫ Have a high pitched tonality. Research done on studying high pitched tonality versus low pitched tonality revealed that the latter is more influential towards impacting people, and is more attractive to women.
- ⚫ #18) DON'T ⚫ Have evasive eye-contact and darting eyes. Eye-contact is one way that close connections are formed. It's especially important to hold eye-contact when leading her logistically; take her hand and fucking lead.
- ⚫ #19) DON'T ⚫ Use fast moving gestures that reveal nervousness - instead of slow moving gestures. **High status body-language is like moving through water.** Fast jerky movements reveal nervousness and overcompensating due to insecurities. Another example: when a woman calls

you from a different direction, don't quickly move your head like rapid fire, but rather slowly move and acknowledge her presence.

- 🌕 #20) DON'T 🌕 Not take up any space at all - which is submissive body-language and reveals weakness. **Women want to mate with the Apex Alpha which is why it's imperative that you exude dominant, powerful, and strong body-language. <u>Be the most dominant man in the room.</u>**

- 🌕 #21) DON'T 🌕 Having monotone delivery and only using 1 type of tone the entire time. A predictable tonality makes one boring to listen to. **Variety is the spice of life.**

- 🌕 #22) DON'T 🌕 Keep a poker-face during the entire interaction - which is part of a larger problem of being too serious and intense instead of being playful and flirtatious. Generally speaking, women at parties would prefer to relax and have light fun banter instead of engaging in intense conversations about the meaning of the universe. **Light conversations precede deep conversations.**

- 🌕 #23) DON'T 🌕 Be in a non-resourceful emotional state which doesn't lead to effective communication. Remember: the emotions that you feel within yourself, manifest themselves in your body-language. **By managing your inner-emotional state, you automatically manage your outer-body-language.**

- 🌕 #24) DON'T 🌕 Keep your head down, and look down. Don't Lean in and be hunching. Stop sitting with bad posture when you're in front of a computer for hours at a day.

- 🌕 #25) DON'T 🌕 Mumble, or stutter your words. Don't speak in a manner that is difficult to understand. If people have to say "what?" That's a strong sign that you aren't communicating clearly.

- #26) DON'T Touch your face during communications, or pace back and forth (both behaviors reveal nervousness). When approaching a woman, if you feel nervous then just imagine how she must feel.
- #27) DON'T Speak quickly like you're rushing to get through your message because otherwise people will stop listening. **Play the pauses.**
- #28) DON'T Always keep a Resting Bitch Face on, and forget to smile. If you're suffering, other people around you will feel those negative emotions and be turned off. This is especially true if you have a anti-seductive habit of complaining and focusing on the negative in life. **Smile from a place of overflowing positive emotions.**
- #29) DON'T Use meaningless filler words that take up time, but don't actually contribute any sort of value. Examples include: "Umm..", "Uhh...", "Like..." **Use pauses instead of filler words.**
- #30) DON'T When engaging in a lengthy conversation, be standing while the girl is sitting down. The fact that she is relaxed, but you're putting yourself in a relatively uncomfortable position just to talk to her is giving away subjective social status. **Alpha males don't make themselves uncomfortable just to talk to girls.**

It's your delivery of the content and belief that the content is worth listening to that carries it enough for women to WANT TO LISTEN TO.

   3. Learn to communicate with non-verbals. In fact, most of communication occurs non-verbally. Practice communicating

with your body-language (including having good facial expressions, posture, and gestures that are congruent to the content) to emphases important points. For instance, when approaching a female stranger on the opening line: it's a good idea to open over the shoulder and to appear like you're about to leave because it has a disarming effect.

BE A LIFELONG LEARNER ✎ .

4. Learn about what's new in the world, and learn more about subjects that are interesting to women. Travel. Do crazy bold shit, so that you can talk about it later. Expand your interests by taking on cool hobbies.

One of the reasons why guys have difficulty talking to girls is because they don't have enough knowledge about subjects that women are actually interested in. Being interesting is simply a matter about sharing insights that bring depth to specific subjects that women care about.

Simply by reading up on subjects such as Yoga, Meditation, Astrology, or Spirituality then you'll infinitely be more interesting to women. Become a relative "expert" in at least one subject that women find interesting by reading at least 3 books on it. This it will put you in a position to be a teacher who can show women the world, and take them on amazing experiences. Teaching her is a technique to establish dominance and get her used to following your lead.

A woman's favorite subject is herself, and a woman is absolutely fascinated by how she is perceived by the world. Hence, making clever observations about who she is and how she presents herself is effective conversation fodder. Become an authority in her world by being knowledgable in the fields of knowledge that she is fascinated by - first and foremost: herself. This is why cold reads (which are statements about who she is as a person) are considered to be chick-crack.

ESTABLISH COMMONALITY ⚔.

5. Look for what you have in common with the woman. **Feelings of (emotional connection) rapport comes from having common interests, goals, and values.** Identify a woman's interests and see if your interests match hers. Discuss insights on topics of shared interest.

    When you're introducing a new subject of conversation, pay really close attention to her non-verbals. Her non-verbals will reveal if that subject of conversation is actually interesting to her, or if she is just being polite.[1] Know the subjects that you enjoy talking about, and that you're knowledgable in. Test different subjects until you get a hit.

    It's also important to keep a mental note of the subjects of conversation that a woman brings up on her own initiative. These are are strong clues that she finds them fascinating. **In general, aim to be a detective in figuring out which subjects of conversation excite the woman who you are dealing with.**

BUILD YOUR ARSENAL OF SOUND BITES ⚔.

6. Keep a player's black notebook. Jot down good lines that have worked for you in the past, and thus empirically shown to generate results for you in the field. The best lines comes from natural spontaneous conversations that you've had with women; the best conversational content is that which is most congruent with your personality and makes sense in the situation that you are in (which is why using memorized pickup lines or routines that you've read off the internet isn't as effective as developing your own content).

    Study comedians and stand-up improvisational comedy to learn the speech patterns and verbal structure that they use to make themselves interesting enough to get millions of people to listen to them. Write down interesting quotes, phrases or expressions that you have heard that you would like to start using in your own personal conversations. The goal isn't to become someone else (even someone who you really admire), but to **adopt their effective communication elements for your OWN PERSONAL STYLE.**

---

1. Establish a woman's baseline (the norm) of body-language behavior to be able to differentiate between a mere Polite Response versus Attraction Response. Women will often give you a Polite Response to avoid hurting your feelings. **You want to focus on the elements and mindsets behind the behaviors that you did which evoked an Attraction Response within the woman.**

MEN AND WOMEN ARE DIFFERENT PLANETS AND THIS IS WHY IT MATTERS.

M<u>en and women are VERY different.</u> You have to let go of the bullshit feminist propaganda, feminists want to brainwash you into believing, that men and women "are the same" and "equal". Men and women are VERY different;

- **THOUGHT.** They *think* differently.
- **BEHAVIOR.** They *behave* differently.
- **ACTION.** They make *decisions* differently.
- **PHILOSOPHY.** The process of how they look at the world (and *interpret* events) is different.
- **SPEECH.** And most importantly: they *communicate* differently.

This is crucial for you to understand because viewing a woman as "a man with a vagina" leads is the equivalent of playing chess with a blindfold on. If you treat a woman in the same exact way that you treat a man then YOUR GAME IS FUCKED.

Don't treat a woman like she is a man - who just happens to have a vagina. Treat a woman differently than you would treat a man because the woman operates on Feminine OS and speaks Womenese, while a man operates on Masculine OS and speaks Manese.

THE TRUTH: WOMEN LIVE ON A DIFFERENT PLANET, AND COMMUNICATE WITH A DIFFERENT LANGUAGE.

FUCK political correctness. This is the truth (be willing to verbalize this 5 times over for the concept to sink in):

MEN COMMUNICATE IN THE MASCULINE STYLE 🏋️, AND WOMEN COMMUNICATE IN THE FEMININE STYLE 💅.

It's problematic when newbie seducers think women ALSO communicate in the masculine style. These clueless guys will interpret a woman's words incorrectly because they fail to realize that she is communicating in the FEMININE which is an entirely **divergent language** and operates based on a different set of variables (e.g. emotion, ego, primal imperatives etc).

The core of problems in long-term sexual relationships is using Manese Tools to understand Womenese.

These clueless guys use the rules of masculine communication ("Manese") to interpret feminine communication and then are left scratching their heads when her actions are misaligned to her words. **They're trying to interpret Womenese with the tools of Manese** (e.g. they think women mean what they say literally, say what mean literally, and uphold their word as honor dictates).

These guys are projecting themselves unto others - erroneously concluding that women are just like them and think just like them. Don't project your own mind unto women because women don't see the world as you do, and don't operate based on the same rules as you operate in. **Don't assume women think a certain way - just because you think that way.**

It's important that we establish the truth immediately that women might as well live on a different planet because of how different they are from men. <u>**Women speak womenese, motherfucker.**</u>

- **The way that a woman shows love to a man** is different than the way a man shows love to a woman.
- **The way that a woman navigates through the world** and makes decisions is entirely different than the way a man operates.
- **The way that a woman communicates** is entirely different than the way a man communicates.

<u>**Women communicate in a secret language that is understand by other women and by men who fuck women.**</u> My goal with this book is to teach you how to decipher this secret language so that you can understand the meaning behind her words, and if you wanted to, could communicate to her in Womanese so she could TRULY UNDERSTAND YOUR THOUGHTS.

Remember: woman want to fuck guys who "just get IT". If she has to explain what she means then inherently the guy "is a loser who doesn't get IT". Being a guy who "JUST GETS IT" implies social proof, social intelligence, and status. Be that guy.[1]

The irony is that women expect a guy to just "get it" without explaining what "it" is. They'll shame men for reading seduction self-help books like this one that reveals the truth about women, while simultaneously reading advice columns in popular female magazine.

WHY DECODING A WOMAN'S LANGUAGE MATTERS

Sun Tzu once said "If you know the enemy and know yourself, you need not fear the result of a hundred battles." Practical knowledge is potential power; applying practical knowledge in the field leads to actual power.

It's a tremendous help to have an acute understanding of "Female OS" operating system to be able to seduce her mind, and unlock her legs. Understand this well: dominating a woman's mind leads to dominating her body.

Mind fuck her, body fuck her and then you OWN HER SOUL. To mind fuck her, you have to understand her mind. **A woman's communication is the window into seeing how her mind operates** - so being able to decipher the truth behind her words is essential.

If you know how a woman thinks, her value system, her belief system, and her emotional-buttons then you'll be able predict how she will behave in response to your sequence of behaviors. **When you understand female nature on a deep level, then women's behaviors become pathetically predictable.** You should understand a woman (and her emotional, psychological, primitive and physical needs) better than she understands herself.

BREAKDOWN ON WHY WOMENESE MATTERS:

- <u>If you understand a woman's deep desires then you will be able to give her that which she values and that will **MAKE YOU INCREDIBLY VALUABLE TO HER.**</u> If you don't understand WHAT her primal needs ARE, then your value offerings will be disregarded as useless. Remember: women are value-consumers and are attracted to men who value-givers. <u>You can't be a value-giver if you don't speak enough Womanese to understand what type of value she deems valuable in the first place.</u>

- If you understand the true meaning behind a woman's communications to you and you're able to acutely read her like a book, then you will be able play her like a violin, and eventually bang the shit out of her. The goal is to constantly progress TOWARDS FUCKING HER IN THE PUSSY - without ever being in the friendzone, wasting time on pointless "going nowhere" perpetual texts, or spending endless dates "getting to know each other". **Put simply: if you know what a woman is thinking and feeling then you'll be able to calibrate your strategy accordingly.**

- <u>A woman is constantly leaving clues on how to effectively seduce her, and these clues can be</u>

picked up by a man who is fluent in Womanese. A woman is constantly sending out signals on what you have to do to FUCK HER, but most men are unable to decipher these clues and as a result of this the sexual opportunity is left uncapitalized.

- **A woman's body-language will betray the truth.** If you simply pay attention to her body-language, you'll be able to identify if what you just did TURNED HER ON (so you can do more of that behavior), or turned her OFF (so you can do less of that behavior).

∿

I'm not going to sugarcoat the truth. Knowing how to have successful sexual relationships with women is an important part of being a man. The moves you make to advance the connection towards sex is based on how you read the woman, and how you read the situation. So it's important that you learn Fluent Womenese **to accurately read the signals that a woman is sending out (while cutting out the noise) to paint an accurate map of reality.**

Nice guys have difficulty exciting women on a primal level because their speech patterns are overly friendly. They fail to understand that women enjoy being teased and appreciate a man who is a challenge. Playing easy-to-get, being a "Yes" Man ☺ , being overly available, being safe/predictable, being a push-over bores women to death. **A woman's perception of the world is based entirely on how she is feeling at in the moment, which is why her perception of reality is volatile and likely to change from day to day.** *If you make her excited then by being anti-nice and having an EDGE to your communication style then she'll form perspectives about you that are positive to rationalize having guilt-free sex. If you bore half to death by being every other average guy then she'll feel anti-climactic and form perspectives about who you are based on those emotions. Remember: a man forms his perception of reality based on logic and empirical evidence, but a woman forms her perspective entirely based on what she feels is the truth based on her current emotional state.*

---

1. It's worth noting that a guy who just "gets it", doesn't have to verbalize what "it" is to women. Just because you understand the dynamics of what is happening, doesn't mean that you have to announce them. On the contrary, it is better to feign ignorance and appear effortless, natural and spontaneous. After all, women would prefer sex being something that "just happens" rather than meticulously planned for. That being said, don't let this become a limiting belief. You can absolutely tell a woman that you want to fuck her, and then fuck her. In fact, you can break many rules of the game and still get the girl in the end, as long as you have confidence, balls, and you're a value-giver.

3

WHY SHE DOESN'T ALWAYS MEAN WHAT SHE SAYS, AND SAY WHAT SHE MEANS

Memes like these depict women as "impossible" to understand and perpetuate the problem. LET GO OF THIS LIMITING BELIEF. While it's not possible to understand a woman 100%, using maxims and general principles depicted in this book: you'll understand enough about women to radically increase your effectiveness in banging pussy.

Why doesn't a woman just say what she mean?

A man's thoughts and intentions are aligned with his words. A man will communicate DIRECTLY. He means what he says, and says what he means. If he has an issue with you, he will confront you directly. A man who communicates indirectly and uses passive aggressiveness is a feminized soy boy.

In contrast, a woman often communicates indirectly. They will say one thing, but mean something entirely different. They will mean to say one thing, but actually say something entirely different. If a woman has an issue with you, she will often be passive aggressive instead of blurting out what the core of the problem is.

- **MASCULINE STYLE OF COMMUNICATION:** Meaning = words.
- **FEMININE STYLE OF COMMUNICATION:** Meaning =/= words.

A woman is often NOT able to accurately represent her thoughts, perspective, intentions and feelings with the words that she uses. What a woman says to you can be COMPLETELY DIFFERENT than the true meaning behind the words. This is due to multiple Distortion Factors such as ego, conformity, peer pressure, anti-slut-defense, fear of confrontation, fear of social discomfort etc. These Distortion Factors will lead to her bending (distorting) the truth

Her words (if taken literally) actually grossly misrepresent her inner-world.

- She'll tell you the truth is "A" but by using your female-decoding intel (because you speak fluent in

Womanese) you will see that the truth is NOT "A" but rather: "B".

- She'll tell you the truth is "A, B, and C" but by using your female decoding intel, you'll recognize the truth is NOT "A", or "C", but rather a harder version of "B".

<u>**To the untrained eye, a woman's words are quite misleading.**</u> Hence, it's vital to take a woman's words through a decoding filter to cut out the bullshit, untangle the misleading statements, and find the truth. A woman's words are more clues about reality (mixed in with a lot of misleading statements) rather than reality itself.

<u>**KEY:**</u> <u>**Train yourself to NOT be bullshitted by a smooth-talker, and to see the RAW REALITY/TRUE MEANING of the SITUATION.**</u> This is a general principle of communication that goes beyond just dealing with women, and extends to dealing with people in general. Don't believe everything you hear. Nor should you believe everything you read.

By swallowing the metaphorical Red Pill and being determined the truth - no matter how painful - you will be in the best position to succeed. Learning to understand the language women speak - Womanese - will enable you to decipher the situation and accurately read the beautiful women in your life. This way you won't get hit with curve balls, and unexpected surprises; for everything a woman does, you would have already anticipated it. **Always be a few steps ahead.**

THE DON QUIXOTE EFFECT

- **MASCULINE STYLE OF COMMUNICATION: Words = actions.**
- **FEMININE STYLE OF COMMUNICATION: Words =/=actions.**

<u>Women can say ONE THING, but then DO something ENTIRELY DIFFERENT.</u>

THE DON QUIXOTE EFFECT: women will often say things based on how they wish the world was - instead of saying things based on how the world actually is. For instance, a woman may tell you things that encourage you to be a nice guy to her, even though those exact behaviors lower her sexual attraction for you. This is because she WISHES that she was attracted to a nice guy, and she'll go as far to even pretend that she is attracted to him; however, she truly fails to understand that she is **disgusted** by NIGE GUYS and NICE GUY BEHAVIORS.

MORE EXAMPLES:

- A woman will claim that she likes nice guys, but then spend all of her time chasing bad boys.
- A woman can claim that she is being confused and frustrated by her boyfriend, but the truth is that his behavior TURNS HER ON. Hence, she can't stop talking about him.
- She says that she really wants you to be sweet to her, but immediately gets COLD the moment you are: then you know that she is TURNED ON by challenging behavior.

If you hear a woman say one thing, but do something completely different: believe the latter. Actions speak much louder than words ever could.

Talk is cheap. Actions show substance. <u>What women claim they want is often different than what they actually respond to on a behavioral level.</u> What women claim they want is often just theoretical and based on fantasies (unrealistic unattainable personal goals), but what they actually respond to on a behavioral level is based on what's practical and the current reality.

<u>Women will often "white lie" to avoid uncomfortable confrontations. It his body-language, micro-expressions, and actions that betray her by revealing THE TRUTH.</u> Learn to not take a woman's words at the surface level, but look to see the implied frames that she is trying to set, the overall meaning of the interaction, and messages communicated by her body-language.

There is saying "people vote with their feet"; this means that a woman's behaviors speaks louder than words ever could. By studying a woman's actions and body-language, you'll quickly assess her true feelings about you. She can be verbally sweet, but if her actions reveal a different story then don't waste your time. <u>OR she can be verbally repulsive but if she's still talking with you and her body-language is receptive then you can still fuck her on that day.</u>

Do more of what works based on a woman's behaviors, and less of what she says she wants (but doesn't respond to on a behavioral level). Live life according to empirical evidence - not according to unproven theories said by women.

THE FIVE FACTORS TO PAY ATTENTION TO ASCERTAIN THE TRUTH WHEN DEALING WITH WOMEN:

- #1) General Body-Language
- #2) Micro Expressions

- #3) Actions
- #4) Honest Signals
- #5) Google her Name, and Look into her Social Media Accounts (to see what kind of person she presents herself to the public - which will reveal who is striving to be)[1]

FUCK feminist propaganda. As mentioned multiple times, men and women are different, and part of that is: DIFFERENT COMMUNICATION STYLES.

By understanding the feminine style of communication, you'll be able to communicate to her in her own language for maximum impact. Hence, one of the goals is to understand Womenese and be able to speak it back to women.

The Masculine Communication Style

Men say what's on their mind. They are direct. Their words have weight to them because there is a code of honor. Men's verbalized thoughts have consistency because logic is consistent. Hence, a man's words are usually aligned to their surface level meaning.

The Feminine Communication Style

Women say what's on their heart. They talk based on how they feel at the moment.

Their words often don't have weight to them because women don't follow a code of honor. Women's verbalized thoughts don't have consistency because emotions are volatile. **She can say that she loves you today, but a few days later break up with you.** What she really meant is that she loves what you represent, the feelings that you make her feel, the value that you give (not you per se) and she'll continue to love you - as long as you continue to give her those things.

4 DISRUPTION FACTORS

It can be hard to decipher the true meaning behind a woman's words because:

- **even the woman herself doesn't understand** half the vomit that comes out of her mouth,
- **women buy into their own bullshit** and can have strong frames themselves,
- **the woman herself will often say things that if taken at face-value are very misleading,**
- **her words are based on how she feels at the moment and how she feels is liable to change.**

A woman actions and words are based on how she is feeling at the moment; just like her feelings are liable to change, so are her actions and words liable to quickly change from extreme to extreme. <u>Women mean what they say but only at that moment - when she feels what she feels then. After all, women live entirely on the emotions of the moment.</u> A woman's opinions and behaviors can change as soon as her feelings change.

In post breakups, women will often rewrite history in a manner that conveniently forgets the positive things that their ex-boyfriend did, and embellishes the negative things that were done.

The key to understanding how women communicate is to understand that women live in the emotions of the moment.

- According to her, if something feels true then it is true.
- If doing something feels good then she will do it.

To communicate on a woman's level then show how being with you is the most enjoyable and fun option for her; demonstrate, don't just explain.

To speak Womenese, minimize logical lectures and instead **communicate in a manner that is emotionally expressive.** Touch a woman's emotional buttons through good story-telling, taboo words MOTHERFUCKER, and a style of communication designed for emotional impactfulness. <u>**Women perceive the world through their feelings, so a style of communication designed to trigger a woman's emotions will be more impactful than a style of communication that is logical and emotionally dry.**</u> This can be hard for high IQ men to implement because they are used to communicating solely on a logical plane, and completely disregard the emotional plane; to go from one world, to another world can be quite challenging for them.

---

1. When looking into a woman's social media account, only casually skim it for a maximum of five minutes - just to get a sense of what her core values are, what her hobbies are, what her ambitions are and so on. It's extremely unhealthy behavior to constantly be checking a woman's social media accounts and to comment with pedestalizing comments like the hordes of other thirsty men. By pedestalizing a woman with your behaviors, you end up pedestalizing her in your heart and mind. Female influencers don't respect their followers and certainly won't respect a thirsty guy writing thirsty comments. Don't waste your life living through the social media posts of someone else. Skim through casually for 5 minutes to gather some actionable-intel (about a woman who you are already communicating with in person in real life) but don't spend any more time than that.

Communication is the act of sending the selected ideas that are on your mind and the emotions that are in your heart, unto someone else. Likewise, it is the process of receiving the ideas that are on the minds of other people, and accurately reading their emotional state.

Communication is a a two-way street. You are constantly sending out and receiving signals from women.

Womenese is the art of understanding the language of women, and being able to read the language of Women. You should have the ability to send out signals (either verbally or non-verbally) in a way that TURNS HER ON, and also understand the signals that she sends out to you in a manner that you are able to accurately read her emotional state, intent, and current sexual interest level in you.

The goal of Seductive Communication is to send out **Sexy Signals** (also known as **Attraction Spikes**) that amplify attraction and avoid sending out **Repulsive Signals** (also known as **Repulsion Spikes**) that decrease attraction.

- E.g. when you casually mention female friends in an entertaining story (where the punchline of the story is something other than the fact that you have female friends), then you'll have effectively sent out Sexy Signals and spiked attraction.
- In contrast when you talk about how lonely you are, and that you haven't been on a date in a while then you've effectively sent out Repulsive Signals and decreased attraction.

Effective communication is important because it is medium of which connections are formed, value is exchanged, and interpersonal goals are achieved. **When you give a lot of value to someone, eventually you become valuable.** After value is exchanged in a mutually beneficial connection over a long period of time, sometimes a relationship is formed. For our purposes, this relationship is of a sexual nature. She feeds on your emotions, attention, and physical pleasure.

Fortunately for her, you're a man of abundance and you have plenty of that which she see desires. You are The Great Prize that she has been born to seek.

Women are value-consumers, and attracted to value givers. **By becoming an effective communicator, you'll be able to generate value from scratch.** I repeat: when you have the right communication skills, you'll be able to create on-command the value that women feed on.

Communication is a medium of giving value.

- Fun is a form of value. You can use communication to entertain, and improve the mood of others - achieving a therapeutic effect.

- Intrigue is a form of value. You can use communication to teach her fascinating facts about her (cold reading, astrology, palmistry, personality type etc.) or her favorite subjects (yoga, meditation, spirituality, her ambitions).

DARK COMMUNICATION

Women are naturally manipulative (and are driven to achieve their personal agenda that benefits them directly - as is human nature in general), **so often the ideas that are they transmitting to you do not reflect reality.**[1]

- 1// Some men have been manipulated by a shitstorm of lies for so long that they've started to believe these lies as reality. This manipulation tactic used by women is known as Normalization.
- 2// Another dark communication tactic used by women, Gaslighting (making a man question his ability to form accurate perspectives of reality) is a tactic that is sometimes implemented by cunning women to take the man a notch down, so he becomes more easy to manipulate.

In Law #1, I discuss one of the primary fundamental concepts to speaking and understanding Womenese: don't always interpret a woman's words literally; ascertain the truth for yourself by using critical thinking skills, and looking at the hard evidence.

---

1. Womenese behavior can be difficult for men to grasp because in the world of men, one's word actually means something substantial. **A man can rely on another man's word because both men abide by honor to keep their word.** Women do not have this notion of honor; they only

"honor" their ruthless opportunistic tendencies. The Truth in a woman's eyes is simply that which supports her personal agenda, that which she feels is true, and that which will help her form connections in the social circle that she finds herself within. In contrast, The Truth in the eyes of a man is based on empirical evidence, and cold logic - without being influenced by the peer pressure of conformity to the same extent.

AN INTRODUCTION TO FEMALE PSYCHOLOGY

Women see what they want to see.

She sees the world through her own personal filter. She'll interpret events based on her own subjective point of view - seeing evidence that confirms with her prior beliefs and ignoring contradictory evidence.

The words that come out of her mouth are merely opinions - even if they sound like convincing facts. Fortunate is the man who doesn't believe everything he hears a woman say, but is skeptical; have your own independent opinion based on:

- critical thinking,
- empirical evidence,
- clusters (multiple pieces of evidence) and
- the assessment of independent unbiased third-party observers.[1]

Frame is your perspective of reality. When your frame is strong, a woman will accept your perspective of reality as her perspective of reality - resulting in a mutual understanding.

Even a dominant woman desires to submit to a more dominant and competent man than her. Even if a woman's frame is very, very strong, your frame must be even stronger. Sometimes it can seem like a woman is extremely certain about her view of reality and it can be tempting to give in to her perspective; even in this moment, your frame should be stronger. Her frame might be IRON STRONG, but your frame should be TITANIUM STRONG.

A woman finds it difficult to respect a man with minimal belief in his perception of reality. The liberal perspective of "everyone is right in their own way" is an ideological virus; **in any interaction, there can be only one version of the truth that is mutually acknowledged, and that version of the truth should be yours. He who controls the frame, controls the game.**

A woman will unconsciously misinterpret events so that it fits in with her prior understanding of reality.

- When a woman is attracted to you then (1) she'll ignore your faults, (2) find excuses for negative behaviors from you, and (3) go as far as breaking her own personal rules for you. She'll be (4) readily available for communication (responding almost instantly to texts), and always down to meetup.
- When she is repelled by you then she'll amplify the nitpicks that she has for you, find ways to reframe even positive behaviors as negative behaviors, and create rules for you to follow - assuming she's still even spending time with you in the first place.

It is silly to follow a woman's lead in life. She simply lacks the ability to reason with cold logic (uninfluenced by emotion), and execute accordingly. **Her actions are based on impulses, what feels good in the moment, and what feels good to**

believe. Establish a behavioral pattern of dominance from the very start. Take control and lead - physically, psychologically, and logistically.

A woman sees the world based on who she is - not so much based on how the world actually is.

Hence, how she describes other people is actually quite revealing about who is as a person. If she constantly focuses on the negatives about other people then this reveals that she is actually quite bitter, and will one day discuss negatives about you. In fact, the words that she uses to describe men in past relationships will eventually be the words that she uses to describe you. **As a side note, inquiring about her past relationships will also reveal the sorts of behaviors and character traits lead her to forming an emotional attachment.**

The words that a woman uses to describe the male/female friendships that she currently has in her life reveal more about her than they do about the people that she is describing.

- She'll discuss traits that she admires and wants to emulate. From this you'll be able to give her solid <u>specific compliments</u> (**based on the person who she wants to be**), and encourage her to pursue her life dreams.
- She'll mention activities that she has done, and experiences that she's experienced that have helped her form an emotional bond with her friends. From this you can get <u>exceptional date ideas</u> (**based on things that she actually really enjoys).**
- She'll reveal seemingly negative behaviors that her close friends have done that has caused her to form a strong bond with them. If she mentions having a verbally abusive ex boyfriend for several years then

she's dropping hints that she bonds through
trauma (also called <u>Trauma Bonding</u>) created
through specific negative behaviors.

Further, the people that she associates with are actually
quite revealing. Women like people that are like them, or who
are like who they want to be. **If she has no female friends at
all, then you should ... RUN AWAY, before you develop feelings for her.** Lacking female friends is a strong sign that she
doesn't have anything of value to contribute to the world, lacks
the basic social skills essential to getting along with others, and
hence doesn't have people around her.

Every woman has a vagina, but not every woman has
something of real value to offer. **If she has female friends
then this is a strong sign that she actually has real value to
offer to the world - enough for other people to want to be
around her.** If she only has male friends then this isn't
evidence that she has substantial value to offer (other than her
body) because the male friends could just be with her for
access to a loose pussy.

**A woman will rewrite her past history based on how she
feels like in the moment.**

99.99% of relationships are temporary in nature. This
phenomenon is largely due to the prevalence of the internet,
social media, dating apps, and dating sites, that has made it
easier than ever before for women to meet men (and hit the
"Next!" Button the moment something goes wrong in their
current relationship).

Even if you get married and raise a family with a particular
woman, divorce or death may occur. Alternatively even in a
marriage, the relationship can be severed in everything but the
legalities. Having the status of being in a relationship does not

necessitate that there is a healthy mutually beneficial connection.

Women will use the status of being in a relationship with a high status man as a way to show off to their peers, and boost their ego; it's not just who you are that matters to her, but what you stand for. **You have to recognize when you are merely a pawn in a woman's game, or the king in her life. Then prioritize her accordingly.**

The savage reality of life is that it is made of a series of creating, and breaking connections. Someone who meant everything to you one day, can suddenly mean nothing to you on the next day. This phenomenon is especially true for women who are biologically hardwired to be able to branch swing to a higher status man - given the opportunity. Hypergamy is a bitch. **One day she loves you, the next day she doesn't care if you're dead.**

Women come and go, but you are with yourself forever. This is why it's important:

- (a) to focus on developing yourself to the fullest,
- (b) use a woman as a practice dummy for the next one, and
- (c) not reveal sensitive information about yourself which can then be used as unconscious blackmail leverage.

Even if the relationship is strong at the moment, your secrets are not actually safe with a woman (including nude photos) because the relationship may fall apart later and then the secrets could be potentially exposed to the world. Don't text something that you wouldn't want to be screen-shotted and sent out to populated FB groups/Whatsapp groups. To keep a secret truly secret: tell no one. Having yourself as an audience should be more than sufficient.

- Your own approval is the only approval that truly matters.
- Draw a sense of happiness from within - without needing to depend on external unreliable factors such as the approval of others.

A woman's word does not mean much because there she does not have the notion of keeping her word for the sake of honor.

While she may say things "I love you", or promise things "We are going to have sex on [specific location]" she may rewrite what has transpired based on how she is feeling like at the moment. This is because women (unlike men) do not have a notion of keeping their word of honor. Their words simply reflect their current emotional state at the time of verbalization. Emotions in general are highly volatile and often based on irrationalities, so they generally should not be relied upon to stay consistent.

Instead of relying on a woman's words to ascertain the future, focus on using her past behaviors to predict future behaviors and creating lifestyle habits that are tailored around quality spending time with you. You want to become an enjoyable habit in her life because that will eventually lead to you becoming an addiction.

PLEASURE HABITS.

Pleasure Habits are some of the strongest psychological forces in the universe; a pleasure related habit can be extremely difficult to break.

- They can be used for the negative (such as smoking habits, drug use habits) that eventually form unhealthy addictions.

- They can be used for the positives (the habit of spending every weekend with you etc) that eventually forms seductive addictions.

THE FAST GIRLFRIEND METHOD

This concept forms the basis of The Fast Girlfriend Method. **The more quality time a woman spends with you, the more emotionally attached she will become.** In the field of psychology, psychologists refer to this phenomenon as The Mere Exposure Effect. To capitalize on The Mere Exposure Effect: the smart seducer will create a Lifestyle Habit for a woman to spend that time with them.

- **Set a time for each day that you will talk to her on the phone.** Create a reason for this such as reading 3 pages of a specific book together. Or talking about how your day went.
- **Set a specific day during the week that you will see her**. The reason for this could be to be Gym Buddies, or to catch local events in the city.

The key is to be consistent and not miss any days - without coming across as needy. If for whatever reason, something comes up and you/her can't make the weekly meetup then be relaxed about it - with a simple "Next week".

- Assume the sale and it will happen.
- Assume that she doesn't like you, and it will often be a self-fulfilling prophecy.

Your assumptions about the degree of your worth, and the degree that she will comply to your requests often become true because ideas are highly contagious.

QT -> Quality Time

Remember: one of the primary goals of communications is to have both parties feel good in the end. When you ensure that the time spent together is of quality - where both of you end up feeling good and both of you have uplifted spirits as a result of the meetup - then a pleasure habit will eventually be formed through enough repetitions.

Pleasure habits eventually form into addictions. **One day when she's expecting you to do your usual meetup, you'll suddenly disappear for a few hours - without explanation - and it will be at that moment that she'll realize that she can't live without you.**

---

1. Don't be afraid to ask for the perspective of male friends. They are emotionally unattached from the situation and thus can give a sharp perspective on the situation.

6

LAW # 49: COMMUNICATE STRATEGICALLY. WHEN ENTERING INTO INTERACTIONS, KNOW WHAT YOUR GOAL IS.

Enter interactions with a purpose in mind.

Strategic communication > mindless communication.

Strategic communication is entering interactions with a *specific goal* in mind, and communicating with the purpose of achieving that specific goal.

- (1) Knowing what you want,
- (2) being conscious of it while engaging in the field (interacting with women), and
- (3) going out of your way to getting what you want (doing specific behaviors designed towards generating results).

are the three most important aspects in getting it. Don't just talk simply to talk. That's a massive time-sink. When you have a goal in mind when interacting with women, you'll communicate with purpose and get more done in less time (maximizing efficiency).

This way you get what you want out of the person who you are dealing with. You'll emerge from situations victorious much better than you were before you even entered them.

Create mutually beneficial situations - where both partners involved get what they want.

- Identify the goal.
- Understand the person's values.
- Show how you can offer the person that which he values.
- Take action to take what you want.
- Both persons involved benefit from the association.

It's worth mentioning that being too outcome dependent can turn women off. Neediness is repulsive to women just like it is repulsive in business interactions. Learn to balance going after what you want, with having fun and enjoying the present moment. Time in field will teach you how to find the correct level of balance.

SUMMARY OF LAW #49

L aw #49: COMMUNICATE STRATEGICALLY

- Enter interactions with a purpose in mind.
- Strategic communication > mindless
  communication.

LAW #50: DON'T BE A SPONGE.

Don't believe everything she says; think for yourself.
Women will say one thing, mean another thing, and the
truth itself can be something entirely different. Don't take
her words at face value; look deeper.

Sexual relationship problems are caused by
miscommunication problems.
You misread the situation, and you misread the
meaning behind a woman's communication to you. She said
"X" and the meaning behind what she said was "Y", but you
interpreted the meaning to be "X" and behaviorally responded
to "X". You failed to see the actual reality of the situation, and as
a result: acted based on an inaccurate map of reality.

HOW MEN SPEAK: X -> X
HOW WOMEN SPEAK: X -> Y
YOU UNDERSTOOD: X -> X

As a man, you will be the most successful when you

operate on an accurate perception of reality - rather than believing in misleading statements women tell you. Knowing the truth is empowering; allowing a woman to put the wool over your eyes is disempowering.[1]

- **1. Don't believe everything you hear.** Look at the evidence including but not limited to: her past behaviors, her present behaviors, her lifestyle, her body language, who her friends are, what other people are saying about her, and micro-expressions. Do these elements confirm her statements, or do they contradict them?

- **2. Don't take a woman's words at face value and interpret them literally.** Only a fool will trust a woman's words as the final truth.

- **3. Use critical thinking skills to separate fact from opinion.** Your mind is one of the most powerful tools in your arsenal for personal advancement, yet most men would rather numb themselves with endless hours of Netflix than think about critical issues currently relevant in their life.

- **4. Learn to be particularly skeptical about information that women give you if they have a personal stake at the matter.** Ask "Does she have something to gain by bending the truth?", "What does she have to gain?" , and "What caused her to say what she told me?" If she has a personal incentive for you to believe something in particular then take it with a serious grain of salt.

- **5. If you are horny, or emotionally invested, then the chances are that the thinking being used at that exact moment is clouded.** The bias can be too high for you to make a rational logical decision. Be

willing to take a walk to emotionally detach from
the situation, achieve a clear state of mind, and then
make a decision based on that clear state of mind.

Critical thinking skills are your most powerful weapon for filtering out bullshit from entering your mind, and only allowing the truth to enter. When a woman loses her ability to trick you into believing a set of fantasies and illusions (designed to maximize the resource extraction that she can get from you), you gain the ability to think for yourself and <u>always take the smartest course of action in the given situation that you find yourself within.</u>

Life is like chess. You have to be able to read the board accurately because then you'll be in the optimal position to make the best move. In life, you always have to be making moves to advance your position.

Understand this right now and right here: the sharper and clearer your understanding of the situation that you are in, the better your decision making will be. This is why it's important for you to not be easily bulshitted and intake false information about the reality that you are in. Being fed false information leads to false actions.

YOU BECOME WHAT YOU READ. YOU BECOME WHAT YOUR MIND
INTAKES AS THE TRUTH.

Women are masters of unconscious and accidental deception, simply by the vast number of misleading statements that they make. Making a move on a woman[2] that forces her to take an action will reveal the truth in the situation, for actions, micro-expressions, and body-language reveal all. Testing a woman by acting upon her is a huge time savor because it lets you quickly read the situation.

A lot of psychological energy is wasted trying to figure a specific woman out. This process of "trying to figure her out" and "see if she likes me or not" can span weeks, months, and in some pathetic cases for years.

It's just smarter to simply make a move.

- Text her.
- After a series of back and forth texts, video call her.[3]
- Invite her out to a local event in the city.
- In the in-person meetup, read her body-language.
- Physically escalate all the way to sex.

By taking action you'll know exactly where you stand, and won't have to waste mental energy doing guesswork.

A woman's operating system follows two codes: "Do what I mean, not what I say", and "Give me what I need, not just want I want."

---

1. Women will often state partial truths to help make lies easier to swallow.
2. Give her a call. Invite her out to a date (local event in the city). Physically escalate on her body. There is a clear binary "yes, it worked" or "no, it didn't work" response to you making a move. "Yes it worked" lets you know that she IS INTERESTED and you should proceed forward in smoothly escalating the interaction towards sex. One of the key concepts in dealing with women is to eject from a state of limbo; force her to make a clear decision towards you, so you aren't wasting psychological energy thinking/planning towards a girl who isn't even sexually available. There's a lot girls out there who are down to fuck you right now as you

are. If you're busy staring at closed doors then you can just miss out on walking through the open doors.

3. FaceTime/Facebook video calls are preferable to just sending out texts because they allow you to see a woman's facial expressions (as well as, signaling with your own facial expressions) during the communication process.

SUMMARY OF LAW # 50

L AW #50: DON'T BE A SPONGE.

- Don't believe everything she says; think for yourself.
- Women will say one thing, mean another thing, and the truth itself can be something entirely different.
- Don't take her words at face value; look deeper.

LAW # 51: SEE THE META-FRAME THAT HER WORDS CARRY.

Understand the implications behind a woman's words. Words are windows into the mind.

Understand the frame that she is attempting to set up. Don't play the game by her rules. Pattern disrupt. She should play by the cards that you deal - rather than the other way around.

Womenese skills is about cutting through the bullshit, ignoring the noises, and using Critical Thinking Skills to decipher the actual truth of the situation. **IT'S NOT ENOUGH TO HEAR JUST THE WORDS THAT SHE SAYS; <u>YOU HAVE TO UNDERSTAND THE DEEPER MEANING BEHIND THE WORDS.</u>**

A woman's belief system will bring about her behaviors. Her words reveal the truth behind her belief system. By changing her beliefs, you'll be able to change the behaviors that stem from these beliefs.

4 questions to ask yourself to ascertain the truth of the situation:

- **Perception lead to thoughts which generates words.** #1) "What do her words reveal about her perception of the situation?"
- **Beliefs lead to behaviors.** #2) "What do her actions reveal about the current state of her belief system?"
- **Actions follow ingrained habits and expectations. <u>A woman is collection of her habits.</u>**#3) "If I allow her to behave in this current matter, what precedent am I setting and is this habitual precedent sustainable in the long-term?"
- **Character creates choices.** #4) Ask "Why did she behave in this manner and what does that say about the kind of person that she is?"

One powerful question that will help you form a clear perspective of the situation is: "Will this matter a year from now?"

The frame that a woman sets about the interaction (through implications of her words) sets the stage for future behavior. For instance: if she says "buy me a drink" she is setting the frame that you are so low-value that you have to pay for her time. If you give into that frame then you're likely to keep paying in the future.

SUMMARY OF LAW # 51:

L AW #51: SEE THE META-FRAME.

- Look at the implications that a woman's words have.
- It's not just what she says. It's the frame that is being set.
- It's not just what she says. It's how she is saying it.

LAW # 52: LEVERAGE SILENCE.

Learn to use silence to your advantage. What you don't say is as important as what you do say. Silence itself is a response. Learn to leverage silence.

Keep in mind that NOT everything a woman says is worth deciphering. Often a woman will vomit an entire series of random nonsense that doesn't matter at all and doesn't have any deeper meaning. Never underestimate the incredible effectiveness of ignoring a woman, as a frame control tactic.

Using silence as a communication weapon will save you from a lot of time-wasting drama. Simply ignoring a woman at the right times will save you a lot of unnecessary pain-in-the-asses. The use of silence is especially golden during shit-tests; when a woman says some stupid drama-creating bullshit then just ignore it, and misdirect her attention to something else - to save yourself the headache.

Ignoring female bullshit will save you a lot of headaches.

What you reward with your attention tends to be rein-forced. So it's important to bring attention to positive behaviors, and disregard negative behaviors (even avoid mentioning them entirely. **Attention is the currency that women crave**, and what you give attention to: will be repeated. This is why it is best to not give credibility to negative behaviors by discussing them .

There are certain specific moments in your communication with a woman where it will be of tremendous benefit for you to be able to understand the true meaning behind the signals that women send out. The key is to pay attention to what matters, and disregard the irrelevant bullshit that doesn't matter.

The 5 Key Rules of Frame Control

- #1) Not everything a woman says is worth acknowledging.
- #2) You don't owe a woman anything - not even closure.
- #3) Not everything a woman says is worth responding to verbally or emotionally.
- #4) Not every question a woman asks is worth answering.
- #5) You can redirect a woman's stupid questions with either a sarcastic answer, or a question of your own.

Learning to say "no" and just ignoring her shit, will save you from tons of female drama and bullshit.

13

SUMMARY OF LAW #52:

L AW #52: LEVERAGE SILENCE AS A PSYCHOLOGICAL WEAPON.

- What you don't say is just as important as what you do say.
- Being silent will save you tremendous time and energy from being sucked into petty drama.
- Attention is the currency that women crave.
- What you reward with your attention tends to be reinforced.
- Bring attention to positive behaviors, and disregard negative behaviors (even avoid mentioning them entirely).

14

LAW #53: ACTION REVEALS ALL.

A woman reveals who she is by her actions. Look at what she does, not what she says she will do; what she does is who she is now, while what she says she will do is who she is striving to be.

W omen are predictable if you know to look at the right **Predictive Indicators**. Most men are clueless because they're using a woman's words as a way to try to predict what she will do - instead of realizing that a woman's words are as cheap as sand on a beach. They merely offer a glimpse into the conflicts of her ever-changing mind. It is action that is king - both in terms of you taking action to achieve your goals, and in terms of predicting a woman's future moves.

The best predictors of a woman's future actions is her past actions, her lifestyle, and her peer-group.

ACTION REVEALS ALL

When seeking to understand women, focus on what she does. Her behaviors are very revealing about who she is. Disregard what she has said, and the reasons that she uses to justify her actions. **Women will say almost anything to get what they want; they won't lose any sleep over using flattery and deception to set you up in the best position to exploit resources from.**

Don't be gullible. Don't trust a woman's words just because she has a pretty face. **Look at the behaviors to see if what she is doing is in accordance with what she is saying.** If you notice a contradiction between what she says and what she does (also known as a Hotspot) then draw conclusions about reality and how she actually feels about you based on what she does.

A fool and his money are quickly separated. If you convey yourself to be a provider then women will use you for resources - even going as far as getting married for that purpose (rather than being with you out of a sincere interest in your personality and physicality). **Look to see if she is behaviorally responsive to spending time with you - even if money doesn't play a role in the dynamic.**

Women will often say one thing, and then do something entirely different. When there's a Hotspot like this, trust the latter for actions speak much louder than words.

Be in the present moment. Observe what is going on, and learn the truth of the situation. Most guys don't even pay attention to what is happening right in front of them because they're stuck in their head thinking about irrelevant concepts (living in their head), and then wonder they don't have an accurate understanding of the sexual marketplace.

15

SUMMARY OF LAW # 53:

L AW 53: ACTION REVEALS ALL.

- A woman reveals who she is by her behaviors.
  Look at what she does, not what she says she will
  do; what she does is who she is now, while what
  she says she will do is who she is striving to be.

16

LAW # 54: THE BODY DOESN'T LIE.

Look at her body-language to see the truth about what she feels about you.

W omen communicate and process information inherently differently than men.
By understanding basic fundamental concepts of how:

- women communicate,
- how they understand what is communicated to them, and
- what changes their mind:

you can utilize this information to control the process. You can manipulate the variables and_hijack the communication process_ to your seductive advantage - making a woman emotionally addicted to being with you, as a result of the techniques mentioned in this program

The goal of learning to be fluent in womanese is to:

- be able to decipher the true meaning behind a woman's words,
- to be able to accurately read a woman like a book,
- to be able to speed read situations,
- to be able speak womense yourself to maximize the impact of your communications, and
- to learn to recognize down-to-fuck signals when they occur, so that you can capitalize on opportunities when they appear.

HOW TO DECODE WOMANESE

Don't believe the egalitarian concept that women are just like men. Women operate differently than men.

Women communicate and process information inherently differently than men.

- 1) Men talk in a masculine style of communication. Women talk in a feminine style of communication. Don't judge a woman's feminine style of communication with the rules of masculine style of communication.
- 2) Men talk to achieve a specific purpose. Women talk just to boost their mood.
- 3) Men will talk to achieve a to exchange ideas related to achieving a specific goal. Women will talk to achieve an emotional high, and to boost their ego. For women: talking is a form of therapeutic catharsis.
- 4) Men meet up to do and get shit done.Women meet up just to talk and experience a good time.

- 5) Men talk to solve problems - talking is a means to an end. Women talk just to talk - talking is an end unto itself.

Don't talk to a woman the same way that you would talk to a guy. Don't treat a woman like a man with an attached vagina. Use the right tools for the right situation.

- 6) Men are direct in their communication style. Women are indirect in their communication style.
- 7) Men state their intentions blatantly and overtly. Women state their intentions subtly and covertly.

Flirting involves showing interest in a woman in subtle ways that keep her guessing. Women get turned OFF and bored if a man gives full validation immediately because it removes the thrill of the chase, and the excitement of figuring him out. Women are TURNED ON by mystery, push/pull (cycling between validation and devalidation), and mixed signals; they get bored when full-disclosure is given. Remember: women value what they work for. The more time a woman invests in thinking about a guy and solving the mystery, the more she becomes hooked.

- 8) Men say what they mean, and mean what they say. Women say one thing, but can mean something entirely different.
- 9) Men talk to convey logical information. Women talk to convey emotions.
- 10) Men talk to exchange facts with one another. Women talk to exchange feelings with one another.

THE EVOLVING CULTURE

The new generation of women is being raised by the internet (TikTok, FB, IG, OnlyFans etc), and this is impacting their ability to effectively socialize with men in a traditional relationship context. A beautiful women who posts photos of revealing clothing for a quick ego boost and is constantly being hit up by men through her IG feed: compromises her ability to pairbond in the long-term. Hookup culture has cheapened the traditional long-term relationship, and has made it easier for women to "hit the next button" the moment something goes wrong in a relationship - instead of trying to fix it.

SUB COMMUNICATION

Don't always take what a woman says at face value. Don't always interpret her words literally. There is more than what meets the eye. Learn to see past the shallow surface level, and uncover the deeper truths of the situation. Learn to see past her behaviors, and into the beliefs that drive her behaviors.

What a woman says, and the true meaning of the situation are often polar opposites. Be a stickler for finding the truth of the situation. Don't be an idiot "Yes Man" agreeing with everything she says just because she has a vagina.

Learning to see the truth behind situations isn't just relevant to dealing with women. It is relevant to how you approach life in general. Don't be gullible and believe everything that you hear - just because it comes from someone who is well-spoken, or has a pretty face. Think for yourself.

WHAT IS SUBCOMMUNICATION?

Subcommunication is the implications behind what a woman is saying[1]. For instance: if a woman asks "How many women have you slept with?" The subcommunication is that: she is interested enough in you to shit-test you. she is testing your composure. she is trying to set the frame that she is THE BOSS of the interaction, and it's your responsibility to answer her directly.

The correct response to a shit test is to agree with the negative and amplify to set the frame that you're a man who *GETS IT* and keeps his social power. After all, women are attracted to POWERFUL men - not men that give away their power. Hence, you respond with a cocky and funny line (instead of getting defensive and justifying yourself to her) like: "You mean only today?" OR "Only 34.5." The key is to always communicate with extreme levels of confidence. Whatever you say, you have to own it 100%.

NOTEWORTHY MAXIM

Deaf men are the best at understanding women because they aren't distracted by a woman's words. A woman's body-language will betray her true feelings, and intentions, but often men are too busy thinking about the bullshit that came out of her mouth to even notice the signals being sent by her body.

THE PRINCIPLES OF FRAME CONTROL (Continued)

- #6) Frame is the mutual acknowledged perspective of the dynamic between you and her. It is the perceived context of the interaction. He who controls the frame, controls the game. You want to be the one who controls the frame, but don't appear like you're like actively trying to do so.

- #7) The stronger frame absorbs the weaker frame; the one who believes more: wins.
- The one who controls the frame, controls the relationship.
- #8) Dominating her mentally leads to dominating her physically. Fucking her mind leads to fucking her body.
- #9) Not everything a woman says warrants a response - or even an acknowledgement.
- #10) Not every question a woman asks warrants a direct answer - or even an answer at all.
- #11) Don't just look at the words she uses, but the frame that she is trying to set.
- #12) Arguing with a woman is falling into her frame. Don't waste time on her petty drama. Win with actions - not debates.
- #13) Being bitter and negative is falling into a woman's frame. Be positive.
- #14) Set the frame with your actions. Touch her body early on, and frequently. Consistently lead the interaction towards sex.
- #15) A woman should be more invested in you than you are in her; this way she is in your frame.
- #16) A woman should be emotionally reacting to you more than you are emotionally reacting to her; this way she is in your frame.

---

1. Generally speaking: the more adept a woman is in sub communicating, the higher the level of social skills she has, and the more Social Capital she has. Subcommunicating is similar to the Law of Say More with Less words. **It's important because one should aim to set the frame of the interaction - without looking like he is trying to set the**

frame. It's easier to manipulate a woman if she doesn't see the puppet-strings that she is being pulled by because she can't resist what she doesn't even know exists. **Aim to have your puppet-strings invisible.** Win through actions - not logical debates. **Often by simply assuming that a woman will behave in a sexual manner (or the specific set of behaviors that you want) and acting in accordance with that belief, she'll just fall into that frame;** in fact, you can get "can get away with" almost anything if you have enough confidence in your perception of reality.

17

SUMMARY OF LAW #54

L AW 54: THE BODY DOESN'T LIE.

- Look at her body-language to see the truth about how she feels about you.
- LEAKAGE explained: Women will bend the truth verbally, but their emotions cause the truth to leak-out through unconscious Body Signals.

18

LAW # 55: TEST HER.

Testing a woman lets you quickly ascertain the truth, without having to put in tons of effort making educated guesses and looking at empirical evidence. This way you won't be wasting time on sexual duds, and won't have to wait for the truth to spill out on its own.

When it comes to compatibility, it's better to find out earlier than letting things drag out. Further, in the context of men seeking a long term sexual partner: it's important to find out if a woman is low quality, or high quality BEFORE you develop any sort of feelings for her and BEFORE you invest a significant amount of time into her.

There are specific things that you can do to test a woman that are mentioned in this book, such as making a specific move on her. She can either go along with your physical advance/accept your date to an invite (which is HARD EVIDENCE) that she is interested in you, or deny it (also which is HARD EVIDENCE). Her actions are binary: it's either a "yes" or a "no", so you'll know exactly how she feels about you through her actions.

Don't fall for the bullshit of a woman saying that she

"doesn't have the time" or other excuses that she gives. Busy people make time for things that are important to them. That's why they are busy in the first place. The extent to which a woman goes out of her way to make time for you shows you the extent that you're important to her (psychologically and emotionally).

If Brad Pitt wanted to see her, I assure you that she would suddenly have a lot of time available.

It's worth mentioning that even if a woman is legitimately busy, if she is interested in you then she will respond by telling you a time that she is available. If she doesn't, inquire about her schedule and create a time based on that.

Understand this: women find time for men that matter to them. If she doesn't make time for you then you are not a priority in her life - to the extent of the high priority that other tasks have. It's time to move on to a woman who values you enough to go out of her way to find time.

On a different note, touching is a key test. **If a woman is responsive to intimate touches then she likes you - even if she appears to be verbally dismissive.** Learn to trust the touching and her actions above all else.

SUMMARY OF LAW # 55

L AW #55: TEST HER.

- Women lie, so men test. When it comes to
  compatibility, it's better to find out earlier than
  letting things drag out - wasting your valuable
  psychological energy in the process.

LAW #56: IGNORE THE NOISE. READ THE SIGNALS.

Read the signals that paint the map, and calibrate your strategy accordingly.

The game of seduction is a continual process of reading the signals that a woman is sending out and adjusting your mating strategy accordingly.

- This means being able to accurately decipher a woman's true thoughts, feelings and intentions - without being mislead by a woman's white-lies, subtle deceptions, and misleading statements. By knowing what a woman is thinking, feeling and what her belief system is then you put yourself in the best situation to seduce her.
- This means being able to accurately understand a woman's true communication to you - beyond what was said on the surface level.

AS A SEDUCER YOU HAVE TO BE ABLE TO READ THE WOMAN LIKE YOU CAN READ A CHESSBOARD - BASED

ON MANY SIGNALS THAT SHE IS SENDING OUT (to paint a map of what types of moves work on her versus the types of moves that don't work on her) - AND THEN CONSISTENTLY MAKE MOVES THAT LEAD TO SEX.

"YOU SEE, BUT YOU DO NOT OBSERVE." SHERLOCK HOLMES

A good seducer is able to observe the accurate reality of the situation, and is able to read a woman's feelings and intentions like he reads a book - by deciphering signals and correctly interpreting the true meaning behind a woman's words.

Use the information that a woman sends out, as a way to learn what works on her (so you can do more of that). For instance:

- If you notice that when you talk about spirituality (astrology, life after death, the butterfly effect, palmistry, PETA etc), she gives POSITIVE BODY-LANGUAGE INDICATORS then this is a clear sign that you should keep using that particular move to form a genuine connection with her. *GREEN LIGHT! GO!*
- If you talk about the technical aspect of your business, and she gives one-worded responses (and other NEGATIVE BODY-LANGUAGE INDICATORS) then you know that, it's time to switch up subjects of conversation. *RED LIGHT! SWITCH IT UP!*

POSITIVE BODY-LANGUAGE INDICATORS

(signals that what your'e doing is working and you should double-down on that particulate move) INCLUDE:

- #1) her eyes light up (including pupil dilation),
- #2) her eyebrows have a brief raise,
- #3) her tonality has a sharp increase (more high pitches),
- #4) she moves closer to you,
- #5) she moves very close to you (past the social zone and into the intimate zone)
- #6) she touches you,
- #7) she positions the direction of her feet/torso towards you,
- #8) she becomes more physically animated,
- #9) she invests more into the conversation (doesn't give merely a polite response to be friendly, and doesn't just give a one-worded response), and
- #10) she is preening (fixing herself up to look more pretty for you),
- #11) she has sustained eye-contact over a long period of time,
- #12) she stops what she is doing in order to pay attention to you,
- #13) when you move somewhere, she'll automatically follow you without saying anything,
- #14) if you tell her to do something, she complies instantly - without hesitation,
- #15) if you ask her out, she says "yes" immediately,

21

SUMMARY OF LAW #56

L AW #56: IGNORE THE NOISE. READ THE SIGNALS.

- The game of seduction is a continual process of reading the signals that a woman is sending out and adjusting your mating strategy accordingly.

22

LAW #57: IDENTIFY HONEST SIGNALS, LEAKAGE, AND HOTSPOTS

The harder it is to fake something, the more reliable of a truth indicator it is. Look for Honest Signals, signals that are hard to fake (like micro-expressions, leakage, and micro-actions).

Words are easy to fake because lying doesn't take much effort. However, actions are much harder to fake because they require a far greater level of conscious effort. This is why a woman's actions are more accurate indicators than a woman's words. Body-language is the hardest to fake of all.

Don't you fucking get it? A woman's body is constantly unconsciously sending out the truth. She can't help it but LEAK THE TRUTH - past her polite filters - through her body-language signals that her body is constantly transmitting.

EMOTIONAL LEAKAGE

Sometimes a woman will try to put on a show for the sake of politeness, but her emotions (are so overwhelming) that they still leak the truth - even if the truth is flashed only for a fraction of the second via a facial expression. This is because the emotions within her are so strong that she's not able to hide them entirely.

HOTSPOT

If you notice a **HOTSPOT (or a contradiction between her verbal communication versus her non-verbal communication) than trust the latter.** A woman's verbal communication is what she wants you to believe and it's within her conscious realm of control (manipulatable). A woman's non-verbal communication is what she actually believes, and for the most part is outside of her realm of control to direct (involuntary).

SUMMARY OF LAW # 57

L AW #57: IDENTIFY HONEST SIGNALS

- The harder it is to fake something, the more reliable of a truth indicator it is. Look for Honest Signals, signals that are hard to fake (like micro-expressions, leakage, and micro-actions).

LAW #58: CONCLUDE BASED ON CLUSTERS.

Identify Clusters.

W omen are constantly leaving clues (signals) on what turns them ON. They're communicating these signals on different mediums - NOT just the words that she says on a surface level. DON'T ACCEPT HER WORDS AT FACE VALUE AS THE FINAL TRUTH.

Look to see if what she says is aligned to the multiple channels of communications that she is sending out. A single indicator pointing towards a particular direction may not be sufficient to form a conclusive conclusion about the woman; however, multiple indicators (CLUSTER) pointing towards the same direction leads to a more decisive conclusive conclusion.

When you are looking to determine the truth about a situation, look for multiple pieces of evidence (CLUSTERS).

11 DIFFERENT CHANNELS THAT WOMEN COMMUNICATE:

- #1) what she is saying,
- #2) what she is doing,
- #3) how she treats you in public,
- #4) how she describes you to her friends,
- #5) how she poses on photos with you,
- #6) the way that she dresses when she is with you,,
- #7) the implications of what she is saying,
- #8) the frame that she is trying to set, and
- #9) the signals being sent with her body-language (including facial expressions, posture, tonality etc),
- #10) how she texts you[1], and
- #11) what she posts about you on social media (if anything at all).

ACCUMULATING INDICATORS TO USE IN CLUSTERS

The digital age has completely changed the way that people communicate. Studying a woman's digital footprint by Googling her name will be quite revealing about her character.

- For instance, if she claims that you're in a relationship with her, but all of her Facebook photos are of her being "alone" (or even worse: you're cropped out) then she is still fishing for a higher status man to come along.
- Another example, if you see that she has dating apps on her phone, then she is still uncertain about a long term future with you.

If a woman rejects you just once then you don't have

enough evidence that she isn't interested. She could have just not been in the mood at that specific point in time. Look for multiple pieces of evidence (cluster) to create a conclusion that is worth acting upon. Put simply: don't make mating decisions based on snap judgments and insufficient evidence.

------

1. If she responds to your text messages FAST and leaves detailed responses then she is INTO YOU. However, if it takes a long time to respond to your texts and they are low-effort texts (one word, or a canned response) then she is not that into you. In general: don't get trapped into becoming a woman's texting penpal. The goal is to always be moving the interaction closer to sex at a reasonable pace. Invite her to a date to an event in the city; then take her home and fuck her.

25

LAW # 59: SIMPLY OBSERVE.

The Map is Not the Territory

This NLP Maxim means is that there is no person on the planet that has a 100% exact perspective on what REALITY ACTUALLY IS. We're all operating based on rough estimations, and that's fine - as long as you don't mistakenly think a woman wants to say "X" when she really meant "Y" because that's a recipe for disaster. You can never see the truth with 20/20 vision, but 18/20 is enough to be hyper-successful with women.

You can't know the exact truth, but you can know enough of the truth to take action successfully. When interpreting a woman's signals, be aware that your interpretation can always have more clarity but you don't need 100% perfect clarity to act. What you don't want to do is fall into The Information Trap of saying, "I can't do anything until I know everything."

OPEN YOUR EYES 👁 👁.

You don't need to be an expert detective in order to ascertain the truth. Nor, do you need to be super high IQ in order to figure out what a woman is thinking and feeling. You simply need to pay attention to what she is doing, tap into your intuition, and look at her body-language (including her tone of voice, pace of speaking, facial expressions and other signaling modalities). **If all you did was simply pay attention then you'll be able to make insightful observations about what** specific strategies work on her, and which ones don't. Ask yourself "What can I learn from this situation to help me in future interactions with this sexy creature?"The problem is that many guys are stuck in their head, and are not even in the present moment to notice what is happening right in front of them.

26

LAW # 60: CALIBRATE, PILOT.

PAY ATTENTION TO A WOMAN'S SPECIFIC SET OF BUTTONS.

Every woman has a specific blueprint on how to seduce her, and its your responsibility to pay attention to her body-language, micro-expressions and clues as to what specific moves work on her. While there are cues that are universally attractive, there are also specific cues that are attractive to specific women; a woman who frequents bars and night clubs will be as responsive to certain as buttons as a career focused women who stays up late studying at libraries to achieve a 4.0 GPA.

When you make a move on her, pay attention to her feedback and use that information to refine your tailored sexual mating strategy towards her. Take the feedback that a woman is giving you and calibrate accordingly.

Learn her buttons. Let go of what isn't getting results, double down on what's working, and be willing to experiment with new tactics to increase the number of effective field-proven tools in your toolkit. Keep a black-book of specific notes about what works with best for each woman in your rotation. On your phone under the contact info, write some basic notes about who the girl is, where you've met her, her favorite topics of conversations, her core values, and places that she likes (for date ideas).

27

LAW # 61: THE TRUTH IS ALWAYS SHOWING.

THE TRUTH ALWAYS SHINES THROUGH.

The truth is out there in front of you. You just have to pay attention to notice it.

If you pay attention you will be able to see the truth. LOOK AT THE SIGNALS and SIGNS; read them and you'll know WHAT THE FUCK IS GOING ON - instead of playing chess blind.

A man who is skilled at reading a woman's body-language can ascertain the truth of what she is feeling at the moment, the level of interest that she has towards him, her intentions, and whether or not she is lying to him.

- Further, he can take specific actions that will force a woman to reveal more information about herself and the situation. For instance, he can come physically close to her. If she pulls back then she's not interested; however, if she stays the same then this is an indicator that she is physically receptive. If a woman is receptive to lower levels of physical

escalation (like a 2 minute handhold) then this is a strong sign that she's receptive to being kissed.
- Another example is if a woman is receptive to drinking from your cup of coffee then she is fine with being kissed (because it reveals a relaxed attitude about sharing your saliva). When you've done this enough times, you'll be able to intuitively sense when the seductive situation is in your favor and you can increase the level of physical intimacy to a more intimate level.

A woman is constantly sending out signals about how she feels at the moment through her body-language (facial expressions, micro-expressions, tonality, body-posture etc), actions, and key phrases. **THE TRUTH IS ALWAYS SHINNING THROUGH.** [1]

Even if she tries to manipulate the presentation of herself, her body and/or emotions will betray her (known as LEAKAGE), and still reveal the truth.

- For instance, she might consciously smile with her eyes, but her feet are pointed at the direction of the door,
- she might be rude verbally (on the surface), but she's letting you massage her butt, OR
- she might be unresponsive to emails/voice messages, but highly responsive to Snapchat DMs, calls and meeting-up.[2]

While a specific signal is subject to different interpretations, when multiple signals (known as a CLUSTER) point to the same conclusion then you form a conclusive insight about her and the situation.

---

1. The truth is always shining through, so how come men don't capitalize on this? Well first of all: many do. But for those that don't: it's because they don't pay attention to the signals that women send out. Simply by paying attention to the truth that is being sent out all the time then you'll have the practical information that you'll need to seduce her.

2. Guys in their late 20s, early 30s might still be used to ancient ways of communicating such as emails, and leaving voice messages. Younger women are communicating on newer mediums such as Snapchat DMs (sometimes to protect their own reputation in the case of having you only as a temporary sexual partner), Facebook Messenger, or IG DMs. If you want to hookup with younger women then get with the times, motherfucker! When you get a woman's personal information I recommend being connected with her on multiple platforms - including FB (where you can see her personal history over the last couple of years). If a woman gives you a throw-away FB account (you can tell that it's fake by the limited number of posts on it) then in the case of men seeking long-term relationships: that's a HUGE RED FLAG.

28

LAW # 62: IT'S NOT JUST WHAT SHE SAID; IT'S HOW SHE SAID IT.

Words are cheap.

Actions speak louder than words. Her actions speak volumes. If there's a contradiction between what she says, and what she does: trust the latter. Words are cheap. Look to see if she walks the talk. Look at what she does - not just what she says.

Pay attention and you'll be rewarded. Don't pay attention and you could miss out on sexual opportunities that are right in front of you.

SIGNS SHE IS DOWN TO FUCK

Major indicators:

- #1) She touches herself in a seductive manner, in front of you.
- #2) She brings up the subject of sex first.
- #3) She brings up "condoms" and/or asks if you have one.

- #4) Mentions that's she's home alone now.
- #5) She takes off any of her clothes.

Minor indicators:

- #1) She shows off her body, and flashes part of her body - making sure that you see it.
- #2) She walks in a way that accentuates her hips and butt.
- #3) She compliments your body, or how you smell.
- #4) Dresses provocatively (more than usual).
- #5) When you touch her body, she doesn't take a step back. When you move in close (past the social space) into the intimate space, she doesn't flinch and doesn't say "what are you doing?"
- #6) She touches you first.

To know for sure, just make a move. Making a move will force a woman to show you the cards that she is holding.

29

LAW # 63: BE A TRUTH SEEKER.

CONDITION YOURSELF TO WANT THE TRUTH AT ALL COSTS.

Seek the Truth - even if it's extremely painful.

While this rule sounds obviously, you would be surprised to find that not all men actually want the truth. As mentioned prior, some men prefer to live in a world of pleasant illusions rather than confront painful truths. Red pills may be empowering, but blue pills taste better.[1]

Men conquer worlds. Women conquer the men who conquer worlds. Don't underestimate a woman's capacity for bullshitting you. Don't accept what a woman says as the truth just because she said it with conviction and confidence. As a man, you have to be able to see past the noise, the distractions, the lies, the bullshit, the temper tantrums and SEE THE TRUTH FOR WHAT IT IS - EVEN IF IT IS DARK AND TERRIFYINGLY UNCOMFORTABLE.

All of Red Pill philosophy is based on the idea of having the truth at all costs - even if the truth is incredibly painful for you to realize and even if the truth shatters your fantasizes of an idealized world. Some men CLING to the hope that their girlfriend is a pure angel because this illusion is erotic, and will deny the truth of the situation to avoid breaking their emotional addiction to having pleasurable feelings towards her. **To be good at speaking Womanese, you must be a good detective about deciphering the truth of a situation - even if a woman is spitting lies into your face.**

ALL MEN CAN HEAR AND SEE WHAT A WOMAN SAYS AND DOES, BUT MOST MEN FAIL TO OBSERVE AND DECIPHER THE TRUE MEANING BEHIND WHAT THEY HEAR AND SEE.

Women will lie at the drop of a hat just to make themselves feel comfortable, and to gain your trust - so as to disarm you - before she exploits you for financial resources. **Some lies can be incredibly convincing because women believe in their own bullshit, and the lies are a long-term play.**

Some lies can be incredibly convincing because society has brainwashed you to "be a gentlemen" and believing "what women say is inherently true". When a man thinks with his dick, he becomes gullible; his lust turns his brain to mush and he becomes easily to manipulate. To be a player you have to always be ALERT and SHARP. DON'T LET YOUR LUST FOR SEX CLOUD YOUR LOGICAL THINKING AND OBSERVATION SKILLS.

Thinking with your dick can ruin your life.

Verbalize the affirmation: "I want the entire truth - no matter how unpleasant the emotional aftermath will be. I WANT THE TRUTH BECAUSE I CAN HANDLE THE TRUTH." While verbalizing affirmations like this may seem a bit "cheesy" and "silly", understand that the unconscious mind is susceptible to self-suggestions. Have a list of personally written affirmations based on sticking points that you want to work on, and read them every single morning. Be willing to change the wording to these affirmations in a manner that emotionally resonates with you the most.

YOU HAVE TO WANT THE TRUTH - AT ALL COSTS. The issue is that some men engage in denial because it makes life more pleasant for them.

MORE TRAPS THAT MEN FALL INTO THE SEXUAL MARKETPLACE (on the theme of COMMON SELF-DECEPTION TRAPS that cause men to misunderstand women)

- 14//They would rather **pretend that a woman is an angel** because it makes falling in love with her easier and the sex much hotter.
- 15//They would rather **ignore their own flaws than deal with the unbearable pain of realizing that they SUCK in certain areas of life.** If a date didn't go well, they'll blame it on the girl rather than themselves (disallowing self-development to occur). It's only when you accept blame upon yourself and take the responsibility of the outcome that you will learn from the situation.
- 16//They would rather **pretend that a woman is really into-them** because their ego can't handle the realization that she isn't interested and it would be a waste of time to pursue this dead-end lead.
- 17//They would rather **pretend that a woman is NOT into them at all,** so they can avoid the uncomfortable fear of escalating. Accept the possibility of rejection when you play the game. When you are fearless of rejection then you will be at your best position to succeed.

- **18//They would rather imagine that they have no potential,** so they don't have to push themselves outside their comfort-zone of binge-watching TV shows while eating junk-food at 3am in the morning.
- **19// THE HALO EFFECT:** They find it difficult to believe that someone who is so beautiful can be so damaged on the inside. They think that outer-beauty necessitates inner-beauty.

———————————————————

1. Denial is not just the Nile in Egypt.

30

LAW # 64: PERSISTENCE SHOWS CONFIDENCE.

DON'T TAKE A WOMAN'S FIRST RESPONSE AS SET IN STONE.

Being able to see past what a woman says on the surface level, and understanding the implications is KEY to being able to decipher her words. What a woman says and what a woman actually means are often two entirely different things. What she says is based on how she feels and her own understanding of her thoughts, both of which are volatile factors. How she feels can easily change from moment to moment, and her own understanding of her thoughts can change too - as she begins to develop a better perspective of how sexy you actually are. This is why a wise man once said, "Don't take a woman's first response as set in stone."[1]

For instance: when a woman says the words "Are you a player?" you misinterpreted the meaning behind her communication to mean "I hate players!! STOP doing the things that are driving me crazy!!" Then you acted in accordance to what she requested, and became the ultimate nice guy: boring her to death. You can be many things to women, but boring is not one of them; being boring is the cardinal sin in a relationships.

You should have accurately read her words "Are you a player?" to mean "What you just did TURNED ME ON!!!" so I naturally followed up with wondering if it was "too good to be true" and "too effective to be accidental". <u>If you accurately deciphered the true meaning behind her words then you would have doubled down on the behavior that spiked her attraction and continued to press that specific button.</u>

Often a woman's first response to your move is just an auto-pilot response that is more based on habit than an actual true response to what you've done. By persisting a bit, you'll convey high levels of confidence and can turn things around. A confidant man doesn't suddenly lose his cool the moment he gets a bit of disinterest from a woman.

A confident man isn't fazed by a bit of disinterest. He'll keep going because he knows that he has a TON to offer women, and he can't even understand that a rejection from her is possible. That's the kind of mindset that he takes with himself to the field, but deep down he knows the score to not waste his time on sexual dead-ends.

---

1. According to science, the more positive time a woman spends with you, the more attracted she becomes to you. This is known as "The Mere Exposure Effect". Hence, by dis-acknowledging a woman's first response and continuing to spend time with her, you can eventually win her over. A confident man isn't fazed by a bit of initial disinterest. Take this advice with a grain of salt. This doesn't mean that you show go full-on verbal harassment situations and get arrested for plowing too hard.

31

LAW #65: CAPITALIZE IMMEDIATELY WHILE THE IRON IS STILL HOT.

When a woman really likes a guy, it is blatantly obvious. If she likes you, you'll know.

This is the answer to the age old question "Does she like me?" You don't need tor read a 300 page book on how to tell if a woman is into you, if she is really into you. The signs are as clear as daylight.

A guy would have to be really insecure to miss them; an insecure guy will generally misinterpret signs of interest as somehow being signs of disinterest because he can't possibly fathom how a beautiful women could possibly be INTO HIM. All that is left is for him to capitalize on the situation, and make something out of it. ONE NEEDS TO ACT ON OPPORTUNITY.

If a woman really likes you, it would be obvious and you wouldn't even ask the question: "Does she like me?" A woman's body-language will reveal the truth; she can't control the signals her body is constantly sending out.

Even if a woman really likes you, if you do nothing then the lead will die. Women have been raised to be passive (although feminists are trying hard to change that). Even if a woman likes a guy, she'll still wait for him to make the move - even if it means losing him in the process. Some women have an ego that is too sensitive, and fragile to risk handling getting rejected, so they won't even try to make a move on a guy (even a guy who they really like). This is why if you wait for sexual opportunities to come to you then you might die waiting. The responsibility for making things happen, and escalation is ON YOU. Don't wait for opportunities. CREATE THEM.

You're the man with a dick, so don't be a fucking pussy. MAKE THE MOVES ON HER. THIS IS YOUR DUTY AS A DICK OWNER.

If a woman gives you bullshit like:

- #1) one worded text replies,
- #2) significant long delays when texting you back (even when you text her back right away),
- #3) doesn't put in significant effort in conversation with you,
- #4) glances away when talking with you,
- #5) doesn't hold eye-contact while talking with you,
- #6) seems easily distracted when interacting with you,
- #7) has a much higher tonality pitch when talking to others,
- #8) spends excessive time on her phone when she is with you,
- #9) is in a relationship with you, but also posts semi-clad photos on IG, texts a lot of male "friends", and has Tinder on her phone,
- #10) is using you as a texting penpal but won't get on a video-call and won't meet up in real life,
- #11) is only interested in spending time with you when you go on fancy expensive dates and doesn't

enjoy basic one-on-one time with you in a simple "free date" (like a date at Washington Square Park)
- #12) keeps digging for info in regards to how wealthy you are (by asking things like "Do you live in a house?")

then she is NOT that into you. Time spent with you is based on what she can get from you, but not because she is actually into your personalty per se. She views you as "he is only good for his money" or "he is only goof for that one thing I can get from him".

Don't take it personally. Just cut your losses and move on to another lead; don't throw more good money after bad money. Don't fall into the Sunk Cost Fallacy of continuing to invest into a losing hand, and continuing to dig a deeper hole. JUST WALK AWAY.

The best way to get over a former lover is to get a better lover, and focus on your personal development. When you find yourself thinking about a former lover, just acknowledge that and without rendering negative judgement about yourself, redirect your thoughts.

LAW # 66: BE AS COLD AS ICE.

Don't take it personally. In fact, don't take anything a woman says personally. Be as cold as ice when calculating and executing decisions.

Women are like children. They say all sorts of random stupid bullshit that they don't understand. Don't take it personally. Life is too short to obsess what someone else thinks. Focus on what you think. Focus on your life goals, and mission.

In the early stages of a relationship, a woman's rejection is meaningless because she doesn't even know you. She isn't rejecting you per se, but she is rejecting the way that you treat her and your specific approach towards her. This is even more reason to not take a woman's words or actions personally.

<u>Seeking a woman's approval is a never-ending blackhole.</u> One day you'll learn that the only approval that really matters is your own. When you give zero fucks about what other people think, you will finally be free to behave as you wish. Truly not giving a fuck is a superpower.

LAW # 67: DON'T PROJECT YOUR OWN INSECURITIES.

REMOVE THE BLINDERS of PROJECTION

The issue is that sometimes a guy will be incredibly into a particular woman and projects his own feelings/thoughts unto her; he thinks that just like he has strong feelings for her, she has strong feelings for him. The guy thinks that she thinks just like him, and feels the way that he feels.

As a result of this blatant misreading of the situation, a guy is likely to waste tons of energy and time pursuing a dead-end lead because he sees potential when there is none. Don't water a rock because you'll waste away that precious water; focus on watering seeds that can sprout into flowers. YOUR ENERGY IS INCREDIBLY VALUABLE; WHY WASTE IT ON NONSENSE? **You wouldn't invest in a stock that is going down, then why invest in a dead-end woman who lacks real potential?** Your time is better spent investing into leads that could lead to something amazing.

Don't play roulette with your life. Your time is more precious than gold. Some guys waste months of their life on an ungrateful selfish woman - who ends up trading up. Invest in women who are "FUCK YES" towards you; don't invest in women who are lukewarm. Life is too short to waste it on women who don't really like you, instead of spending time on women who are crazy about you.

Don't make lots of assumptions about the women and the dynamic between you and her, without taking the time to look at the evidence. When you have multiple pieces of hard evidence pointing towards a single conclusion (also known as a CLUSTER: see Law #4) then trust that conclusion - even if your emotions and feelings are painting a different picture entirely. <u>**No matter how you feel, trust the cold hard evidence.**</u>

Nice guys have the tendency to make lots of assumptions about their low self-worth and lack of options; these assumptions tend to become a self-fulling prophecy. If a guy thinks he can't get girls, he won't. If he thinks his situation is hopeless, it will be. YOU HAVE OPTIONS, MOTHERFUCKER; JUST OPEN YOUR EYES.

TRUST EVIDENCE OVER EMOTION. THINK WITH COLD HARD LOGIC UTILIZING FACTS AND STACKING OBSERVATIONS; DON'T THINK WITH YOUR DICK AND MAKE IMPORTANT LIFE DECISIONS BASED ON THE ARBITRARY WHIMS OF EMOTION.

Overconfidence can lead to self-sabotage. If a guy thinks every single girl is down to fuck then he will waste a lot of time pursuing girls who aren't excited about picking up what he is putting down (value exchange compatibility) instead of pursuing girls who are excited about what he has to offer. Filter for women who are picking up what you are putting down - buying what you are selling.

IF YOU HAD TO ASK THE QUESTION "Does she like me?", YOU ALREADY KNOW THE ANSWER.

Seducer: "Hey, lets head out and meetup on Sunday for Coffee. I know this great place in XYZ location."

Woman: "I have to think about it" or "I'll get back to you on that!"

If a woman says anything but a certain "yes!!" then she's not into it. When a woman is DOWN then it is clear that she is DOWN. If you're missing those signs then the answer is an acute "I'm holding on to you - just in case I can't find another guy. You're my backup guy" or has your name saved as "free food" on her phone.

34

LAW #68: MAYBE IS NO.

Anything that is not an enthusiastic immediate "yes" (such a 1-2 worded verbal response that beats around the bush) is a lukewarm "no".

While it's certainly possible that you can eventually turn a woman's mind around - considering how susceptible women are to having their mind changed - it should be noted that not every woman who you can get, is worth getting. Some women are too much of a hassle (carry too much emotional baggage) to be worth the effort to fuck, when instead you could have just focused on women who are a lot more interested in you (your effort would have a more bang per unit of sweat). Instead of trying to win over a disinterested woman, wouldn't it be a better use of your time to focus developing stronger connections with interested women?

35

LAW # 69: SILENCE IS NO.

Not saying something is saying something. Silence means "no".

A woman doesn't want to be seen as a bitch, so instead of confronting you directly (like a real man would), she'll use a passive-aggressive approach and simply ignore the issue entirely. Understand that no response is a response in itself. <u>In other words, not saying anything is saying something; silence communicates a signal.</u>

Understand that when a woman is crazy about a guy, she can't stop talking about him. If she really likes something, she won't shut up about it. The passion is overwhelming for her, and she wants to share it with the whole world! The fact that she is able to stay silent about the matter simply reveals that she doesn't care for it.

Guys will sometimes fall for the Polite Response Fallacy thinking that if a woman is simply friendly to them then she is interested in a romantic manner. The truth is that the woman was just being friendly because she was raised to get along with others. Simply experiencing friendliness is not sufficient enough evidence to conclude that a woman is into you; look for enthusiasm, excitement and eagerness (Ask "Is she really into the interaction?" or "Are these elements missing?"). Does she light-up when she is with you, or are her responses "forced" monotone - almost robotic?

∼

HOW TO SCREEN FOR HIGH INTEREST

Life is short and then you die. Choose who you allow into your inner-circle carefully.

YOUR TIME IS WORTH MONEY. A lot of womenese is about being able to decode which women are really interested in you (and to what extent), so that you can continue to invest in them and not waste time/psychological energy on women who are not interested in you. Run tests on women to gauge physical devotion, and then prioritize them accordingly.

An important concept to understand in regards to speaking womenese is that women have been conditioned to be polite. Even if a woman doesn't like you in a sexual way, she'll still be friendly because this is how she was raised. Guys can read too much into a woman's friendliness and misinterpret it as signs of attraction. **This is why you want to MAN THE FUCK UP, and MAKE A MOVE to force a woman to show the cards that she is holding.** Touching a woman in an intimate matter is the fastest way to test sexual receptiveness. A woman being conditioned to being friendly, and a woman's desire to ease social tension/uncomfortable confrontations is what leads her to using softeners - white lies that are there to make the guy feel better about himself and to minimize the chances of aggressive intimidation.

THE SPECTRUM OF HONEST SIGNALS

While this is a book about speaking womenese, it's worth pointing out that a woman's words ultimately can't be trusted. They are merely a glimpse to a woman's emotions and intentions AT THAT EXACT MOMENT IN TIME but these can change quickly. More reliable indicators of a woman's behavior are her past behaviors, her character, her body-language and her present actions. Women will lie at the drop of a hat, so the truth is best deciphered through more than just a woman's words - such as looking at what SHE DOES, and the clues dropped by her body.

36

LAW # 70: PASSIVITY IS YES.

A woman is brainwashed by society to be acted upon - more than to act on a man. Hence, she spends most of her life just waiting for men to make moves on her. The most she can do is send clues and signals that she wants to be acted upon (for instance she can "accidentally" expose parts of her body for you to notice her, she can "accidentally" brush up against you, or she can "accidentally" say something overtly sexual), but her ego is too fragile to being the one who does the acting.

If a woman isn't saying "no" (in terms of her body-language, her actions, and words) then the answer is "yes" and you should keep advancing the interaction towards sex.

If she is still showing up on dates and spending time with you (despite the sexual frames that you set and frequent touching that is happening) then assume that is interested in being with you.

An absence of a "No" is a "yes" because if a woman wasn't interested in you then she wouldn't even be responding to you at all. She would just ghost, block, or tell you to leave her the fuck alone.[1]

1. The exception to this rule is in a work environment where a woman may be just being friendly to create a pleasant vibe. In that particular case, look to see if she goes beyond basic friendliness and her basic obligation to being polite into doing something "extra" for you. If she does then she is interested.

LAW #71: IDENTIFY HER CORE VALUES, AND THEN FEED IT BACK TO HER.

Identify a woman's core values and communicate them back to her. Establish commonalities of interest.

- Learn to identify the feeling that is valuable to her that is behind her words. Reflect that type of feeling back to her.
- Learn to identify specific trance words that she uses. These are specific words that have special meaning to her. If you use these same words, you'll maximize impact.
- Identify her specific body-language and feed it back to her through Mirroring and Matching.

Look for what is valuable to her. Then show her that you've got plenty of that in your life. By being a part of your life, she'll get access to more of which she values.

LAW #72: SHE SHOULD BE SUCKED INTO YOUR WORLD, MORE THAN YOU ARE SUCKED INTO HER WORLD.

Speak her language, but don't be sucked into a woman's world. Bring her into your world.

While you will occasionally speak Womense to have a maximum impact on her, you want the woman to be more drawn into your world than you are drawn into her world for the sake of sustaining attraction. A woman should be pulled into your perception of reality more than you are pulled into her perception of reality. <u>Even a dominant woman wants to submit to a more dominant and competent man.</u> For instance: in religious circles, this would mean being a spiritual leader that will guide a woman towards living a life of greater meaning based on shared values and shared philosophies.

Don't spend too much time deciphering the true meaning behind a specific woman's words for the sake of gaining access to her pussy. If you pedestalize a woman in your mind, you will pedestalize her with your actions. Needy behaviors are very unattractive to women. Being more invested in her than she is in you leads to low status behaviors. The goal is to improve your skills with women in general - not just to get a specific woman that you want.

HOW TO SPEAK WOMANESE

- Men talk about abstract concepts and philosophy. Women talk about gossip, food, and shopping - down-to-earth concepts. A woman's favorite subject of conversation is herself, and about things that directly benefit her. When talking show how what you're saying relates back to her - even if you're talking about yourself.
- Men care about how what you say teaches them something new - the educational value of your communicational content. Women care about how what you say makes them feel something - the emotional value of your communicational content.

39

LAW #73: STACK VALUE.

Attention from high status men, good emotions from a positive vibe, and fun from enjoyable experiences are forms of currency that women value. Bring the value.

Women live for good emotions. What she cares more about than anything else is how you make her feel. She feels what you feel because of mirror neurons. When you feel AMAZING, then she will feel AMAZING. Feel joy and enthusiasm for life; let that joy overflow in your words.

Communicate to women from a place of overflowing positive emotions, benevolence, and high energy. Focus on uplifting her mood, and pumping up your emotional state. Press her emotional buttons. When you understand the maxim that girls just want to have fun, then a lot of what a woman says/does will start to make sense.

- Men focus on the content and the rational arguments behind issues. Women focus on the context and how issues make them feel.

- Men are moved by solid logical arguments - that are backed by evidence. Women are moved by stories, and appeals to emotion.

Be a giver of value. Stack it.

40

LAW #74: PLAY ALONG THE FANTASY SHE DESIRES TO SEE. LEVERAGE SEXY STEREOTYPES AND HER IMAGINATION.

ADOPT A SEXY STEREOTYPE THAT IS BASED ON THE DESIRES AND WANTS OF THE DEMOGRAPHIC OF THE WOMAN THAT YOU ARE INTERESTED IN. Understand that women respond to their imagination of you more than the objective reality of who you are.

AS A MAN, YOU CAN BE MANY THINGS TO WOMEN, BUT YOU CANNOT BE BORING. Being boring is the cardinal sin of dealing with women. Playing it safe, predictable, and nice is playing it boring. You need to START TAKING RISKS in interactions with women. Be edgy. Polarize. START DRIPPING WITH PERSONALITY. Bare your naked soul. Express yourself freely and fully. Take on intriguing hobbies and develop an identity that women will find interesting.

Womenese isn't just about what you say directly to women. It is also about who you are as a person. Your identity and behaviors communicate signals to women that speak louder than words. For instance: if you live a spiritual life dedicated to a Higher Purpose then those set of behaviors communicate waves of messages to women about who you are, and the values that you stand for (much more than words could possibly articulate). In stark contrast, if you live a fast life of cracking the code to beating casinos at their own game and drive a Ferrari, then you're likewise communicating on a medium that sends shockwaves to a woman's system - even without speaking a single word. The key is this: your clothes, accessories, body-language, facial expressions, actions and lifestyle are sending messages to women in a silent language that creates IMPACT in their minds.

A woman who is attracted to you is unconsciously visualizing herself as part of your life. Her fantasies feel very real to her. A woman's imagination leveraged properly can be a powerful seductive weapon. Hence, posting exciting photos that showcase your lifestyle will have a woman imagining what it would be like to spend time with you.

I'm going to take a moment to reveal an extremely powerful tool to make a female friend desire to go on a date with you. Don't underestimate the power of this. Describe in detail a date that you took a woman to. Make it exciting. Have it include emotionally intensely fun activities. Hype it up to the moon. Paint a vivid picture of an enjoyable experience. After a couple of days break up with this "woman" (it's better for her to be a real woman who you want to date a long time ago, so the details of the date will be real - instead of made up). Invite the girl you like on a date and she'll say "yes" because she's already been pre-seeded into the idea that dates with you are fun. Using stories and third-person framing are powerful ways to subtly set the right ideas into a woman's mind.

~

3 SPECIFIC EXAMPLES ABOUT PREEMPTING WOMEN'S BEHAVIORS WITH COUNTER MEASURES DESIGNED TO AMPLIFY HER LEVELS OF SEXUAL ATTRACTION FOR YOU

1// For instance: if you know that asking a woman for permission before doing something will lead to her losing respect for your authority and ultimately resulting in lackluster sex, then you'll immediately cease this beta male behavior. Be a leader - not an approval seeking simp. Be a decisive warrior - not a soy boy. A woman wants to look up to her man and be challenged (she resents being able to control a man like she controls a dog on a leash), so put yourself on a pedestal and don't ask her permission to do what you have to do.

2// Another example: if you know that saying "sorry" sets a precedent for more simp like behavior, then you'll avoid unnecessarily apologizing for your existence. Apologizing is beta male behavior that comes from insecurity and self-doubt (the exact opposite of confidence). Expressions of self-doubt and weakness absolutely disgust women - just like men are disgusted by expressions of obesity. Stop saying "sorry" (a word that kills the vibe), and start OWNING IT. For every word that comes out of your mouth, own it 100%. When dealing with women, exude extreme confidence. YOU ARE A FUCKING 10, SO ACT LIKE IT. YOU ARE THE PRIZE TO BE WON, SO BEHAVE ACCORDINGLY.

3// Final example: if you know that giving into a woman's Boundary Pushes, only reinforces her negative behavior and will embolden her to progressive violate even more of your boundaries, you won't stand for her bullshit. The more disrespect you put up with, the more she will disrespect you in the future. Here is a savage truth about women: they don't respect men that they walk all over - like a doormat. If a woman treats a man like shit, she will start to believe that he is shit. Don't be a fucking pushover. Don't put up with bullshit. Call women out on their BS behavior. Communicate boundaries clearly, and be willing to walk if they're violated.

STAND UP FOR YOURSELF. LOOK OUT FOR YOUR-SELF. This is a job that only you can do for yourself because women are too busy obsessing over themselves. Everyone is out for his own skin. It's imperative that you look out for YOUR SKIN

Women see the world through emotional lenses. Feeling something is true is enough for it "to be true" - to a certain extent. Women use their emotions as a guiding system to navigate their behaviors, and to "perceive the world with". Men that are able to express themselves on an emotional level will be able to communicate in a manner that really resonates with women.

41

LAW #75: A WOMAN'S VIEW OF THE WORLD REVEALS WHO SHE IS.

A woman sees the world as she is - not as the world is. This is true for you, as well.

You see the world as you are. How you interpret a woman's communication shows a lot about who you are. An insecure guy will interpret everything a woman does in the negative, but a confident guy will see everything as signs of interest. Ironically: having the habit of confidently reframing of a woman's actions is a self-fulling prophecy. If you convey the frame that she likes you, she will often fall into that frame.

THE SIX LAYERS OF COMMUNICATION

- **I. The first layer is the truth of the situation (also known as The True Meaning).** This includes: the truth about her wants, the truth about her desires, and the truth about her feelings towards you.

Example: The truth of the situation is that her body craves sex, she enjoys the sexual pleasure of clit stimulation, but she can't actually verbalize these truths directly because society will judge her for it (and her fragile ego won't let her). You can decipher the true meaning of the interaction by judging her actions. If she is spending a lot of time with you, SHE LIKES YOU. If she followed you into the bathroom, she is DOWN TO FUCK RIGHT NOW. If she got on your bed, she is DOWN TO FUCK RIGHT NOW.

- **2. The second layer is a woman's perspective of the truth;** what she believes is the truth (a subjective diluted understanding of the true meaning). Most women do not have a well-developed understanding of their nature, so their perspective can be very off. This is especially true if a woman is stupid because she relied heavily on her looks to get by in life (and thus her perspectives can be remarkably off).
  Example: the woman engaged in self-denial that she enjoyed being FUCKED HARD in the bathroom because this would make her feel very guilty. She REALLY BELIEVES THAT SHE IS AN INNOCENT PURE ANGEL because her ego wanted to feel important and she buys her own bullshit. She wants to have sex but she can't admit this to herself because it would maker her feel slutty.

- **3. The third layer is a woman's intention and purpose of communicating her perspective (The answer to "why did she this?").** Sometimes a woman will have the intention of just talking to improve her own mood and meet her social needs ("talking for the sake of talking" - a stark contrast to men who talk for a specific purpose). She aims to convey her beliefs - either partially or entirely (what she means to say) - as a means of self-expression. Other times: it's for a specific unconscious goal such as mating, unloading her feelings, or virtue signaling. *Example: she said "I thought we weren't going to have sex" so as to take the blame off herself and then be able to justify things to herself as "it just happened".*

- **4. The fourth layer are words that she uses to convey what she meant to say** . The words she uses can be very misleading to what she means to say, her perspective and to the actual true meaning. *Example: she said "I thought we weren't going to have sex" taken as face value implies that she doesn't want to have sex with you. Her words are not good at conveying her intentions and desires, so this leaves guys confused.*

- **5. The fifth layer is what she didn't say.** Guys can be so focused on what she DID say that they fail to pay attention to what was NOT said - which leaves clues to the reality of the situation. *Imagine this: her pants are down, and you took out a condom. She says "I thought we weren't going to have sex". She didn't say "NO!" You should have put on the condom and fucked her hard because complaining about getting FUCKED is not the same as saying "I don't want to have sex with you." Sometimes women give token resistance because they get TURNED ON by the man being aggressive. Needless to say, if she did explicitly says "no" or "stop" then don't proceed and get a rape charge.*

- **6. The final layer is that which you understand her words meant about her intention, her perspective of the True Meaning, and what you concluded the true meaning was based on observations/deductions.** For clueless guys playing a broken game of telephone, it's no wonder that they misinterpret the true meaning of the situation and behave in ineffective ways towards women. *Example: the guy thought her words meant "I don't want to have sex with you", so he ended the sexual interaction - without tapping into his killer instinct to fuck close and seal the deal.*

SUMMARY OF THE 6 LAYERS OF COMMUNICATION

- **Layer 1:** She desires to fuck. This is clear by her actions. She went into the bathroom and took off her pants.
- **Layer 2:** She mistakenly thinks she doesn't desire a good fuck because her self-denial is preventing her from seeing the truth. However, even if she thinks sex with you is "wrong" or "sinful", she still went into the bathroom with you and isn't walking away because HER BODY CRAVES THE EXCITEMENT/PLEASURE YOUR DICK PROVIDES - hijacking control of her actions.
- **Layer 3:** Her intention is to say something to make herself feel less slutty/guilty by taking away (from herself) the responsibility about what is going to happen.
- **Layer 4:** She complains by saying "I thought we weren't going to have sex" - giving herself catharsis in the process.
- **Layer 5:** She didn't say "NO", "Lets not have sex", or "Stop". This gives passive permission. This also conveys an unconscious desire to be "swept away" in the moment by Alpha Male Leader.

- **Layer 6:** The guy takes her words at face value and doesn't give her the physical value that her body craved. An opportunity is lost because he didn't understand womanese, and didn't read the overwhelming series of "DOWN TO FUCK" signals.

42

LAW #76: MOST OF COMMUNICATION IS UNSPOKEN.

Control the controllers.

A woman's words reveal a window of insight into her belief system and character - which ultimately drive her behaviors. It is prudent to look past the surface level of her words, and aim to see deeper meaning behind what she said (or didn't say). Likewise, don't just look at her key actions (or lack of) but the decode the reasons that motivated these actions. When you understand the variables behind the drivers that drive her behavior then you'll be able to manipulate these variables to influence her behaviors.

A woman's communication style and behaviors are influenced by multiple variables. When you gain an understanding of these Influential Variables, then you will be able to manipulate these variables and redirect the outcome to an outcome that you seek. Control the controllers.

What are the variables that direct a woman's behaviors?

- Her ego
- Her emotions
- Her unconscious mind (and set of beliefs within there)
- Her conscious mind (and set of beliefs that she is aware of)

Game is manipulation and manipulation is game; if you have a problem with that then this book isn't for you. OWN YOUR IDENTITY AS A PLAYER OF THE GAME - or get played by other people in the network of game players that is the world. You are in the game of life - whether you want to acknowledge it or not. STOP FUCKING DENYING the fact that life is a game and one is far more likely to win in this game by being proactive, being aggressive in executing goals, implementing conscious strategies, and following a plan of action than if he takes on a passive approach merely hoping to get lucky.

SUMMARY OF KEY POINTS:

Men and women are VERY different physically and psychologically. As a man, it is a grave error to project yourself unto women; just because you think and operate in a certain way does not mean that women share your sentiment. Just like men and women are VERY different physically and psychologically, they are VERY different in their communication styles - both in regards to how they transfer over information to others, and how they process information from others.

In fact, the difference is so vast that women might as well be speaking in a different language - namely Womenese and the subject matter of this book.

I. LOGIC VERSUS EMOTION

- **Men focus primarily on communicating logical information.** He says what he believes to be true based on facts, evidence, careful thought, and logical deduction. Just like logic is consistent, a man's word tends to be consistent.
- **Women focus on communicating emotional information.** She says what she feels like is true. Just like emotion is volatile and tends to embellish reality, a woman's word tends to be volatile and inaccurate.

II. DIRECT VERSUS INDIRECT

- **Men tend to be more direct and confrontation.** They aren't afraid of social awkwardness and tension, so they'll generally have no issue with saying something negative straight to your face. Hence, they will say what they mean and mean what they say.
- **Women tend to be more indirect and passive aggressive.** They actively seek to avoid social awkwardness and tension, so they'll say something negative to others about you through gossip (also known as SOCIAL AGGRESSION). When talking to you, they will sometimes say what they mean, and sometimes NOT say what they mean. Instead of

saying what they mean, women will use white lies to bend the truth, and leave clues about what they mean. Women expect men to "just get it" without blatant explanations - even when she can be quite misleading.

III. PRACTICAL VERSUS MERELY CHATARSIS

Men are inherent problem solvers, achievers, and focus on communication as a medium to GET SHIT DONE. In contrast, women aren't thrown in to the world with a stark need to build their sexual market value, so their communications are focused on talking just to talk, and to uplift each other's spirits. Men earn their sexual market value; women are born into their sexual market value. Men generate value; women protect their value. Men focus on achievement; women focus on enjoyment.

～

It is worth noting that generalizations such as this are not binary and should not be interpreted into extremes. We are dealing with spectrums. There is some feminine in the masculine and vice-versa. For instance: men are not cold machines executing based on 100% logic and 0% emotion; men's judgement is influenced by emotion just like women but to a lesser extent than women. These are generalizations, and like generalizations there will be anomalies and different people will be on different ends of the spectrum.

In general, women are far more emotional than they are logical, but a woman's upbringing will influence her psychology. In certain cultures such as the western culture in the U.S., individualism and achievement are heavily promoted as valued ideals; thus, women in this demographic will be more focused on achievement than traditional cultures that hold traditional values as sacred: women stay at home to take care of the children, clean and cook - while a man is the breadwinner. Context and a woman's upbringing should be taken into account when decoding Womenese.

There are three primary goals of learning to speak Womenese:

- **1) To create an immediate feedback loop.** A man who is able to decipher a woman's body-language will know instantly if what he is doing is working by reading her positive body-language. Likewise, he will know instantly if what he is saying is NOT working by reading her negative body-language. This immediate feedback loop is valuable information to improve your game. The problem is that men that can't speak Womense can't decipher the clues constantly leave on how they desire to be seduced.
- **2) To understand what a woman value,** so as to be able to give them that specific form of value and become a valuable emotional commodity in her life.
- **3) To be able to quickly read the signals that a woman is sending out that she is DOWN TO FUCK, so that you can capitalize on the opportunity immediately.** Likewise, it's important to read the signals that a woman is not sexually open, so that you can stop wasting your time. It is more efficient to focus on fucking women that are more promiscuous in nature than it is to attempt to emotionally and physically persuade a virgin into intercourse. As a man, don't take the role of savior;

unless you're married to her and in a mutually beneficial long term relationship, it is not your responsibility to save her from herself. Women use a man's Savior Complex as a means to exploit him for his financial resources.

43

LAW #77: THINKING AND MAKING DECISIONS WITH YOUR DICK CAN DESTROY YOUR LIFE.

Don't think with your dick.

Not matter what a woman says, or does: remain calm, composed, and unaffected. Getting emotionally attached to what a woman says makes you susceptible to making stupid decisions. Lust turns a brain to mush; when you are horny, your thinking is clouded. Thinking and making important life decisions with your dick can destroy your life. If you have to make an important decision, take a walk around the block to clear your mind and think from a position of clarity - rather than giving in to the heat of the moment.

While not everything a woman says is worth your time to decipher, there are key moments which will be quite revealing about who she is as a person, what she finds valuable, and what turns her on, that is worth your time to pay attention to. **Everyone sees what women do, and everyone hears what women say, but not every man observes.** When you know what to look for and have a refined process of observation then women's bullshitting doesn't stand a chance; you'll come out with the truth every time.

Women are not "pure angels"; they "smart girls" and they have an agenda. Don't underestimate a woman's capacity to bullshitting and manipulating you - especially if you are a man with resources. While you can take time to understand what she said versus what she means to say, understand that the truth of the situation may be entirely different. Always confront the truth regardless of how painful it is for you to acknowledge because a man as it his best with an accurate map of reality - rather than a map of reality based on self-denial and pleasant illusions. In fact, the entire premise of the Red Pill is to accept the reality for what it is NO MATTER HOW PAINFUL THAT REALITY IS and act accordingly.

T**he game of seduction is like flying an airplane. The smart seducer is able to read a woman's signals and then make micro-adjustments to his seduction plan based on the signals that he is getting.** Double down on behaviors that get excited positive body-language, while minimizing behaviors that get a flatline negative (or null) body-language response. It is not prudent to play the game of chess with a blindfold on. It's worth your time to pay attention, read the woman, read the situation, and make CALIBRATED MOVES that make sense in the context. A tailored seduction approach based on a woman's specific blueprint on how to be seduced will work much more than a cookie-cutter "same thing for everyone" approach.

W**hat a woman says, and what she meant to say can be entirely different.** She might not have the word power to accurately articulate the thoughts that her on her mind. Even if she was more articulate, she might not understand the situation and herself enough to be able to portray an accurate perspective about what is happening. Further, what a woman says is often entirely based on how she feels at that exact moment which is subject to change; hence, the classic maxim "Change her mood to change her mind." The conclusion behind these truisms is that a man it's your responsibility to have your own unbiased independent opinion about her, the situation that you're in with her, and the dynamic between the both of you. While a woman's words provide clues about the reality, they should not be taken at face value - especially if it is her first response to your move.

LAW #78: WOMEN ARE INDIRECT CREATURES.

Women will go to far lengths to avoid social awkwardness, and to generate good emotions for themselves. Billionaire dollar industries are built on a woman's need to feel important, and filling that need with physical possessions.

Most women have been conditioned to be polite. They'll avoid direct confrontation for fear of retaliation from men, and being perceived as a "bitch". In general, women will go to far lengths to avoid feeling socially uncomfortable around people they just met. I'm going to repeat this again because it is an incredibly important principle in understanding how women communicate; <u>women will speak in a manner to create good emotions for themselves and will go to far lengths to avoid social awkwardness.</u> Hence, women will communicate rejection in subtle ways - nicknamed Soft Rejections - to preserve a man's ego and the feel-good vibe. These Soft Rejections can take the form of made-up excuses that shift the blame on to her.

As just mentioned, most women have been raised to be friendly to others. In the case of a woman seeking revenge, she'll use indirect social aggression such as gossip, spreading lies, or reporting a man to authorities with false/greatly exaggerated accusations (behavior encouraged by the #MeToo movement). Fortunately for men in the U.S., rape is incredibly difficult to prove in a court of law (just save the texts and don't write self-incriminating field-reports on the internet); however, unfortunately for men, even a false accusation is enough to smear one's good name and reputation in work circles.

In the case of men, direct confrontation clears the air; however, in the case of women, passive aggressiveness for former perceived wrongs can span years and generate a toxic vibe. In the case of the latter, it is much more efficient to start a new relationship with a new woman than to invest mountains of effort to healing a woman's emotional baggage; when you have game skills, women become as abundant as sand on a beach. Instead of wasting days upon days trying to fix things with a damaged woman and a broken past with you, it's more efficient to just meet a new woman to start afresh.

Communication is the art of transferring the thoughts that are on your mind, and the feelings that are in your heart to someone else. **The meaning of communication is how what you said was interpreted.**

It's not just just the content of what you said that matters, but the overall implications and frame that was set through a verbal medium. A frame is the mutually acknowledged perspective of the situation. The seducer's goal is to set frames that are conducive to sex occurring; it is beneficial for the seducer to learn how women process information, so that he can be effective in setting seductive frames.

45

LAW #79: CREATE A MUTUAL UNDERSTANDING THAT SEX WILL HAPPEN.

Set frames that are conducive to sex occurring. The mutually acknowledged perception of reality sets the stage for the actions that will occur.

For instance, the frames:

- #1) Sex is normal."
- #2) "Sex is healthy."
- #3) "We enjoy the pleasure our bodies give."
- #4) "I am the authority and dominant leader in the interaction."
- #5) "Meeting new people is fun, and engaging in physically intimate acts is fun too."
- #6) "It is not our role to negatively judge others. Why people engage in "nasty" sex is not our business."
- #7) "Life is short. It's important to enjoy momentarily pleasures while we're still alive."

are far more conducive to sex occurring than "Sex is dirty. Sex is sinful. I feel shame and guilt for feeling sexual gratification. You (the woman) are just as much of an authority as what we are going to do as I am." To speak Womenese, take a few moments to deeply reflect on how a woman's mind operates.

LAW # 80: BE AN INSIDER.

BE THE GUY WHO "JUST GETS IT".

I ronically, women expect a man to "just gets it" - without it being directly explained to him. For a woman to explain the seduction and communication process to a man, would ruin the experience for her and takes the man out of the category of "just gets it" and into the category of "socially inept incel who "is too stupid to be worth my time. Don't take it personally; this is just the brutality of nature at work. A woman's sexual nature can be incredibly sexually ruthless and efficient; this is why women resent men reading books like this that attempt to inflate a man's sexual market value.

As a man, you want to "just get it" without explaining the dynamics of the situations to the woman because that would take away from the natural spontaneous feel of the conversation. Behave from a position of effortlessness - even if you are carefully executing a plan that leads to intercourse. Just because you understand what is happening doesn't mean that you should explain it to her; men that "just get it" don't feel the need to tell the entire world about it.

LAW #81: A WOMAN'S MIND HAS AMBIVALENCE.

Why do women say one thing, but mean something else?

There is someone within you who is seeking to sabotage you - all the time. This person lives with you, and knows everything about you because... *drum roll* he is YOU. This is the weaker version of you that is always present. Life is a constant struggle between the weaker version of you, and the stronger version of you. This battle is ongoing 24/7. It is the version of you that you FEED WITH ACTION that grows stronger with time. If you keep taking POSITIVE ACTION in the direction of your goals and vision, then you'll naturally create a POWERFUL MOTIVATIONAL MOMENTUM THAT INSPIRES MORE ACTION.

Eventually, you'll reach a point where all you do is WIN ALL DAY LONG. You become addicted to the high that you feel that comes from WINNING.

The weaker version of you feeds an endless supply of excuses and reasons why you should be easy on yourself. "Sleep in because it's cold outside" it whispers in your mind. "Don't work out today because you need a break. You've had a long day" it continues to tell you. "There is no point in approaching and making moves on women because you are disgusting" it whispers in your ear - baiting you to go easy on yourself. When a man believes in these limiting beliefs and excuses, they have greater power over him. The more one believes in a limiting belief, the more it limits him. The key is to not identify with the weaker version of you, but to identify with the stronger version of yourself.

You can recognize this internal struggle by differentiating between what you feel like doing and what you actually want to do. You FEEL like binge watching a show on Netflix, but you WANT to read a book on business. You FEEL like not approaching and making a move on the beautiful woman that you like because it's scary (and your ego can get hurt in the process of playing the game), but you WANT to develop the TAKE ACTION HABIT and a fiery momentum, so you approach anyways. You FEEL like emotionally exploding to a verbally insulting comment a woman says to you (shit-test), but you WANT to stay composed and not waste your time on her petty drama. The aim is to develop enough self-control to be able to do that which you WANT TO DO, and that which is aligned to your GOALS - rather than what you FEEL LIKE DOING in the present moment and that which gives into your desires for instant gratification. SELF-CONTROL IS CHOOSING TO DO THAT WHICH IS YOUR HIGHEST PRIORITY - even when you really don't feel like it.

Psychologists refer to this as the battle between the ego, and the super-ego. The ego is about having instant pleasure at all costs with complete disregard to the consequences. The super ego is about having a higher purpose and keeping your actions attuned to that which is beneficial for you in the LONG TERM. It is the ID (namely YOU) who decides between the two sides: good versus evil - or in this case, beneficial versus self-sabotage.

I'm bringing down these concepts to make a few vital reasons:

I.

Firstly, I want to emphasize the fact that YOU ARE AT WAR. Don't you understand that power isn't handed out for free? It is SEIZED. It is TAKEN. Don't you get it? One doesn't magically land on the APEX OF THE SOCIAL STATUS HIERARCHY by accident, or luck. It takes years of conscious self-development, overcoming inner-weaknesses, internalizing WINNING MINDSETS, and creating sets of lifestyle habits that lead to results - such as the TAKE ACTION EVERY DAY HABIT. You have to be your own best friend and coach to constantly inspire yourself to get the fuck outside of your comfort zone, and take EXTREME RADICAL ACTION TO GET MOTHERFUCKING RESULTS TODAY!!!

II.

Secondly, within here is a key concept in understanding how women communicate. It is **ambivalence**.

Women can hold contradictory ideas and have mixed feelings and issues about people.

This is why women will often say one thing, but do something entirely different. This is why women seem to consistently shift their perspectives and change their mind from one extreme to another extreme. This is the answer to the age old question: "Why do women say ONE THING, but actually mean something ENTIRELY DIFFERENT?"

The answer is: even women don't fully understand themselves. They are plagued with confusion. They are often torn themselves between doing what their super-ego wants versus doing what their ID wants.

One of the reasons why women will have contradictory ideas in their mind is because of an unconscious need to keep their options open. They don't want to give a HARD NO, because that can burn bridges, but they also don't want to give a HARD YES because of reservations. A woman is a flawed creature that is still trying to get by in life - in anyway that she knows how.

You sit down deep in your couch scratching your head pondering hard "WHY did she say XYZ, but later say ABC? Why did she promise she would do XYZ, but later completely flipped to ABC? Why is there no consistency in what a woman says, to what she actually believes and does on the next day?" It is because there is a significant inner-conflict within a woman that includes confusion. Put simply: she hasn't figured herself out, and she doesn't even know what she truly means.

You're probably thinking "Okay, so I can't trust what a woman says to be the final truth because what she says may not be aligned to her beliefs, and even if what she said is aligned to her beliefs, those beliefs can change. If I can't trust what she says then what am I supposed to do? How can I predict a woman's behaviors enough to not lose my mind in dealing with her? How can I play the game if I can't see the chess board, and have some consistent expectation about how my opponent will move his chess pieces?"

The secret is to understand that women are actually predictable, but not in the way of looking at their words and expecting women to keep their promises. Talk is cheap - even among men. Talk is even cheaper amongst women who will promise the world, and then do nothing. Women will say almost anything to avoid uncomfortable tension that comes from social confrontation, and this is why they can't be trusted; a woman's talk is the cheapest of cheap because she will easily bend the truth to avoid feeling uncomfortable in the situation (and then do something entirely different when you're not around, or flip her perspective by 180 degrees when she feels differently). The way to predict women is to look at that which is far more consistent and predictable: a woman's habits, life-style habits, and character.

If you understand human nature, you'll understand women and will come to realize that women are pathetically predictable.

48

LAW #82: IN HER MIND: IF IT FEELS TRUE, IT IS TRUE.

Women think with their emotions.

Don't take anything a woman says personally. If a woman says something insulting to you: don't take it to heart, because she is just expressing how she feels at the moment, and her feelings are subject to change. Change her mood to easily change her mind. Women "think" with their emotions; feeling something to be true is enough to make it true.

Don't accept a woman's first response to you to be set in stone. As she gets to know you more, her attraction levels can spike, her mood will change, and behavioral response can shift radically in a positive direction.

∼

- Men care about the truth. They have an open mind to accepting the truth - as long as sufficient evidence and a strong argument is presented. Women care

about believing what feels good. They see what they
want to see, and believe what they want to believe.
- Men process the world based on facts. Women
process the world based on how they feel.

Miscommunication happens when a man uses his
information based perspective of understanding the
world to interpret and attempt to understand a woman's
emotional way of communication. Miscommunication
happens when men use their manese language to understand
womanese.

- Men make their decisions based on what they want
and cold logic (which stays the same). Women make
their decisions based on what they desire and how
they feel at the moment (which can change).

WOMANESE IN RELATIONSHIPS

- Masculine men have a stronger frame (perception)
and lead a woman - mentally, logistically, and
physically. Submissive women have a weaker frame,
and submit to a man's view of the world - following
his lead. Even if a woman's frame is very strong, your
frame must be STRONGER. A confident man has a
bullet-proof frame. He inspires women to follow his
lead. A submissive woman is a sexual woman.

- When expressing a problem, men want solutions.
When expressing a problem, women want empathy.

49

LAW #83: A WOMAN'S MIND IS MALLEABLE.

A WOMAN'S PERCEPTION IF MALLEABLE. If a man has intense conviction in his beliefs then his belief system will overtake a woman's belief system.

A man with in intense conviction in his high worth, and the high worth of what he has to offer will create a positive emotional experience for women.

By changing a woman's perception of your worth, you'll directly impact whether she says your sexual advances are "cute", or "creepy". If she sees you as an APEX ALPHA MALE at the top of the social hierarchy and socially proofed (other women want to fuck you, and men want to be you) then she'll use language patterns that are suggestive of you guys getting together. But if she sees you as a broke loser living with his mom with no future, ambition and no friends then she'll use language patterns that are suggestive of you not being with her. It's the difference between her saying "us" or "you". While a woman's language patterns offer a glimpse into her world, it is prudent to take them in context with other signals that a woman sends out such as her body-language, facial expressions, present actions, past actions, the actions of her close associates, social media presence, her reputation, and the enthusiastic (or lackluster) recommendations of her references.

SOFT REJECTIONS

Women use socially acceptable ways of rejecting men like:

- "I need space",
- "I have to think about it",
- "I need some time",
- "I'm not ready for dating right now",
- "I have to figure things out for myself right now",

because they want to avoid being seen as a bitch, and they want to bypass burning bridges. Understand this other Red Pill Truths about Women:

- 1. A WOMAN WILL GO FAR TO AVOID FEELING SOCIALLY UNCOMFORTABLE.
- 2. A WOMAN WANTS TO KEEP HER OPTIONS OPEN.
- 3. WOMEN ARE SOCIAL CREATURES AND CARE GREATLY ABOUT THEIR POSITION IN THEIR SOCIAL CIRCLE.
- 4. A WOMAN USES A MAN IN HER ORBIT, LIKE A MAN USES A TOOL IN HIS TOOLBOX.

Hence, women will say things that are intentionally ambiguous and non-committal, so as to not say "yes", but also not give a definite "no". This way you'll stick around just in case she needs to use you in the future. While men stick to values such as HONOR and doing the right thing, women stick to solipsism and being ruthlessly efficient. It's more ruthlessly efficient to lead a guy on with false hope, so as to use him in the meantime for his resources than it is to give a HARD REJEC-TION and burn the bridge. For some guys who are conditioned to pedestalize women, these hard truths to accept as reality, but you must UNDERSTAND THEM TO BE THE PAINFUL TRUTH, so that you can free yourself from enslavement to pussy. Pimp - don't simp.

The problem with SOFT REJECTIONS is that they are incredibly misleading for the vast majority of men who don't speak womenese. They also prevent guys from learning from their mistakes because a woman puts the blame of sex not occurring on herself. Finally, soft rejections lead guys to waste more time on a sexual dead-end instead of using their incredibly valuable time to generate more leads, or to invest in women who are actually worth it.

The key Red Pill Truth to understand is: DON'T BLAME A WOMAN FOR WHERE YOU ARE IN LIFE. Where you are in the present moment is based on the actions that you have done in the past. Where you will be in the future is based on the actions that you are doing in the present. You have to understand this incredibly important concept: YOU ARE THE ONE TO BLAME FOR YOUR CURRENT POSITION IN LIFE. If you wasted thousands of dollars on a woman who never really care about you, and only cared about the financial resources that she could extract from you then that's your fault. No one told you to believe her lies. No one told you to believe affectionate words such as "baby" meant that she really likes you. No one put a gun to your head and told you to spend your valuable resources on an ungrateful women would would trade-up the moment opportunity presented itself and conveniently rewrite history. YOU ARE THE ONE RESPONSIBLE FOR YOUR ACTIONS.

Likewise, if a date didn't go well then it's YOUR FAULT. And it's on you to figure out what set of behaviors or things that you said implied low social status, so that you can learn the lessons from the experience and implement a refined mating strategy in the future. The problem with soft rejections is that guys might not view them as rejections, but rather actually believe the woman when she puts the wool over the guy's eyes with "You're an amazing guy, and you'll find someone! I'm just not dating right now." This advice is misleading. It is more efficient to tell the guy exactly which specific set of behaviors he has to work on to improve his dating strategies in the future, but women won't reveal this because of their general principle of avoiding confrontation.

50

LAW #84: A WOMAN IS A SLAVE TO HER PERSONALITY.

A woman is a slave to her personality.

She doesn't exercise her freedom of choice and willpower to break out of human nature. If you understand a woman's character you'll be able to predict her behaviors. For instance: a woman of low social economic status is more likely to do drugs, steal, and have questionable morals than a woman of higher social economic status.

THE 4 KEYS TO BEING ABLE TO JUDGE A WOMAN'S CHARACTER

- ☞To ascertain a woman's future behaviors look at her <u>previous behaviors.</u> To see a woman's future, look at her past. To predict what she will do, look at what she has done.
- ☞To ascertain a woman's character look at <u>how she treats people who can't do anything back to her</u>. It is easy to be nice and friendly when it is

convenient, but look to see how she behaves when it is not convenient to do "the right thing".

- **To see what kind of person she is, look to see <u>how she treats her father because this is how she will come to treat you</u>.** A woman has been conditioned to treat her dad - the authority figure - in a specific way, and she will come to treat you in the same manner. Likewise, pay attention to how she treats people who are close to her because if you become close to her (through being engaged in a long-term relationship with her) then chances are that she'll treat you in the same way.

- **To ascertain a woman's level of promiscuity, gauge how many other instant gratification behaviors she engages in.** If you notice that she's engaging in instant gratification behaviors such as tattoos, piercings, weed, alcohol, mild altering drugs, revealing clothing, petty theft then these are signs that she has the kind of adventurous

51

LAW # 85: A WOMAN CAN'T BE TRUSTED WITH YOUR LIFE.

A woman's words can't be trusted because of a woman's inherent biases to knowing the actual truth of the situation.

People engage in self-denial because fantasies are more pleasant than truth. Even if you accurately interpret what a woman meant to say, and her view of the world, you still have not uncovered the true reality of the situation. How a woman views the world and the actual True Reality of the situation are different things. A woman's perspective can vary from 10/20 to negative 10/20 (what she believes can be the exact opposite of the reality) because there are psychological barriers (self-denial, confirmation bias, emotions, ego, distractions, etc) that prevent a woman from seeing things clearly.

Women are highly emotional creatures. Their perspective of how the world works is heavily subjective and based on their emotions; her judgement is clouded by her desires. <u>A woman will behave according to the world she WISHES she lived in - rather than confront the incredibly painful reality that the world is much more grim than she imagines.</u> This is similar to the story of Don Quixote; an aspiring knight would so emotionally attached to a perspective of reality that gave an emotional high that he convinced himself that the world was according to how he felt like - instead of looking at the RAW HARD COLD FACTS. It is painful to acknowledge certain truths about the situation, so women will just ignore those truths and pretend everything is sunshine; denial isn't just a Nile in Egypt. Denial of the truth is a psychological phenomenon women use to protect their emotional state and egos; it happens more often than you realize.

52

LAW # 86: DON'T FALL INTO THE HALO EFFECT TRAP.

Don't be fooled into thinking a woman is an angel of purity.

Women have an agenda - even if that agenda is unconscious. If a beautiful woman is with a guy then you better believe that she is getting some sort of value from him. Understand this very clearly in your mind: the moment a woman stops getting value from a guy is the moment that she vanishes from the face of the earth and focuses on other guys. Women are value-consumers, and will stay with you as long as you are a value-giver; fortunately for them, you are A MAN OF ABUNDANCE and have tons and tons of value to offer. You have a TON TO OFFER to any woman who enters into a sexual relationship with you. BE A GIVER OF VALUE.

It is crucial to be able to know the type of things that women value, so as to be able to give women value consistently and thus have them around in your life. It takes an understanding of Womenese to be able to provide the type of value that women find valuable; after all, what is valuable to you as a man, is not necessarily what is valuable to a woman. BURN

THIS INTO YOUR BRAIN. Women value three things more than anything else in world and these three things are: good experiences, good emotions, and happiness. As a man, you are essentially a drug dealer dispensing the chemical high of good feelings to women - over a long period of time. She is using you for good emotions.

Guys misunderstand women because they take what they say through a literal medium, instead of reading the vast number of other signals that women are constantly sending out (such as facial expressions, body-language, tonality, a woman's past actions, and current actions). Womenese is ultimately understanding what a woman means to communicate, the truth of situation, and being able to communicate effectively. To truly understand what a woman means, you have to look at the entire CONTEXT of the situation (this means being aware of where you are in the environment, the dynamics of the situation, and key signals that a woman is sending out); likewise, to speak womenese effectively, you should take the CONTEXT of the situation to account.

53

LAW #87: CONTROL THE
CONTROLLERS PART 1

Treat women as they are - not as you wish them to be.

You have a conscious mind, and an unconscious mind - with the unconscious mind being far more powerful. Most of your daily decisions are run by the unconscious mind that is operating in the background. By changing the unconscious mind, you'll be able to change thousands of micro decisions and behaviors that happen on auto-pilot throughout the day. 🕶 **A woman's unconscious mind is a primary driver of everything that she does in life.**

Another factor that influences a woman's decisions is her emotional state. Women are highly emotional creatures. They'll make important life-changing decisions based simply on how they feel at the moment. Women live in the emotions of the moment. This goes so far as women deciding certain things about the world are true simply because it feels true.

- By changing how she feels, you'll change how she views the world and how she will behave.

- By changing her unconscious mind, you'll likewise change how she behaves.

54

LAW # 87: CONTROL THE CONTROLLERS PART 2

Y OU ARE A COMMODITY
Create the frame that you are The Prize to be won. This frame is set by your actions, words, and body-language. You are the one who screens women to see if they're worth your time - not so much, the other way around. You are "VALUABLE ASSET" in the interaction. When this frame is set, then women will be uncontrollably attracted to you.

So what is the great secret to spiking your perception of high worth - to the point that women are dripping wet?

The secret is: SELF-PERCEPTION.

What does self-perception have to do with attracting women?

EVERYTHING.

Self-image influences external behaviors, body-language, and signals.

Women will view you based on how you view yourself. If you think you are a shit women will see you as a shit. If you see yourself as THE SHIT then women will likewise see you as THE SHIT. Know that you are GOLD, and that what you have to offer women is GOLD.

It's female nature to use a man's level of confidence as a shortcut to assess his competence in the game of life, because a woman's lifespan is too finite to give each man a full chance. A woman's time is too limited to give each guy a complete try, so she relies on Honest Signals and other indicators to see if the guy has "got the goods" that she is unconsciously and consciously looking for.

When you have an intense conviction of your high worth then it shows!

The body is always communicating by sending out external signals. Women automatically decode these signals that you are sending out about your worth, and then either get TURNED ON (by Displays of High Status) or turned off by displays of low status. The key is exude Sexy Signals, and avoid sending out Loser Signals. It's not just about hyping yourself up; it's also about not talking yourself down - even with self-deprecating humor.

You're wondering "Okay so I have to come across as IMPORTANT. I have to send out signals that show me as IMPORTANT, and avoid sending signals that make me seem IRRELEVANT. But how does one go about doing so? Does one memorize a list of 100 different sexy signals and then consciously send out all 100 - a nearly impossibly overwhelming task?"

There is one incredibly powerful shortcut that is the equivalent of consciously implementing 100 seductive behaviors. This self-development technique can be quite literally LIFE CHANGING.

By changing your beliefs to "I am THE GREAT CATCH", then you'll automatically have the behaviors that reflect this mentality. Beliefs = behaviors. Merely having the self-perception that you are a high-status man leads to behaving like a high-status man; likewise, having the self-perception that you are a fucking loser leads to behaving like a low-status man. Changing 1 internal belief leads to automatically changing 100s of behaviors associated with that belief.

The same is true in regards to controlling a woman's behaviors. By changing her belief system, you change the behaviors that go along with that.

1 BELIEF = 100+ BEHAVIORS

For instance: imagine knowing that you have a million dollars in your bank account. Simply that knowledge automatically changes the course of hundreds of micro behaviors. You don't need to read a list of 43 techniques in a hypothetical "How to Have Rich Man Energy to Make Accelerate the Networking Process" ebook, because you'll automatically have Rich Man Energy. When you have the belief system of a man who is naturally confident with women then you'll effortlessly do sexy confident behaviors. Being extremely confident won't just attract women into your life; it will also attract rich men into your life - effectively allowing you to network and create mutually beneficial business arrangements. Game skills are transferable, motherfucker!

<u>Women naturally gravitate towards men they see as being of ultra high worth, so by creating this perception that you are high worth then you'll be able to fuck an ocean of pussy.</u> Confidence is incredibly sexy to women. While you look for a young fertile body, a woman looks for high levels of confidence; she's screening for your level of self-belief, and using that as a shortcut to assess your worth in the culture and society she's born into.

High worth means different things to different types of women. Being a spiritual guru will open an ocean of pussy.

DEVELOPING TRUE CONFIDENCE

This self-perception of high worth comes from:

- - having self-respect,
- - having standards,
- - being willing to walk away,
- - being able to set clear boundaries,
- - standing up for yourself,
- - being assertive,
- - having competence in skills valued in society, and
- - having your life shit together.

I t goes without saying that: if you are an unemployed broke guy who:

- - lacks grooming,
- - dresses like shit,
- - doesn't have a future,
- - doesn't have an established peer network tribe of winners,
- - lacks a basic self-care routine,
- - smells,

then your confidence levels won't be significant. Confidence comes from life competence. If your life is falling apart, then consider taking a break from pickup, cutting off losers, cutting off low ROI activities, cutting off time-sinks (social obligations) and putting an extremely concentrated intense effort GETTING YOUR SHIT TOGETHER NOW!!

Allowing yourself to be treated like shit lowers your own

confidence levels. Likewise, giving into social inhibitions compromises confidence. When you don't approach and make moves on a beautiful woman that you like then you are sending signals to your unconscious mind that you are UNWORTHY.

THE UNCONSCIOUS MIND WANTS PROOF - NOT JUST PROMISES

The unconscious mind is always listening. If you treat yourself like a priority then self-esteem will develop. If you treat yourself like trash the insecurities will develop. Behaviors are more influential in creating your personality than affirmations, self-suggestions, pep-talks, and research. You create your personality with every choice that you make.

<u>The perception of high-worth is created by being dominant in interactions. Lead, lead, and do more leading.</u> Being dominant creates a perception of status and confidence. Lead a woman towards a path of victory. According to researchers, simply behaving in a dominant manner makes people (women included) believe that you have greater levels of competence.

You don't need to compensate with money to make a woman like you. In fact, using money to attract a woman has the opposite of its intended effect. You'll end up attracting gold-diggers who don't give a fuck about you; they just care about the money that they get from you. The emerging sex (if any at all) will be lackluster or fake at best. The goal is not to have sex with a beautiful woman at all costs. The end goal is to have sex with a beautiful woman who is interested in you for you (your personality). There are levels to the game.

While men are attracted to physicality, women are attracted to personality and status. Unfortunately for women, their beauty is locked by whether or not they have won a genetic lottery of looking pretty. There is a limited flexibility that a woman can do about her own beauty - outside of plastic surgery. In stark contrast, through intense conscious consistent development, a man can raise his status within society, improve his game skills, and improve his abilities to generate value that is valued by women.

LAW #87: CONTROL THE CONTROLLERS PART 3

PROJECTION

Women think that other people are just like them. Hence, how she describes and talks about other people is actually quite revealing about her own character. If she says that all of her friends are sluts then she probably has a promiscuous nature too. If she mentions that all of her boyfriends (sexual relationships) are assholes then you know what you have to do. ;-)

THREE MORE WAYS TO KNOW HER CHARACTER

Keep in mind that you can tell a lot about a woman by the places that she visits, the company that she keeps, and what she talks about.

1// For instance: if she's a student in the New York Police Academy then understand that it takes a certain kind of person to choose that kind of career path; for whatever reason, there's a lot of cuties going down this path (speaking from personal experience as one who attended New York Police Academy meetings). Another example: if she's a studious college student then it's clear that politically correct success is a value in her belief system. In general, you're more likely to meet higher quality relationship material young women in a college campuses than in bars and clubs; the former is focused on long-term success, while the latter is sunk in a lifestyle of perpetual instant gratification.

2// Likewise a woman's choice of friends reveals a lot about her character because it is human nature to become just like the people that you hang out with. If all of her friends are males then she probably doesn't have much to offer besides a used vagina. If she did have something of more substance to offer then she would actually have female friends. People with similar interests, goals and value CONNECT together. Hence, finding commonalities with the woman that you're interested in is an essential strategy in seduction. The value system of her friends is likely to be her value system too because of Group Think; women are like sheep following what other sheep do.

This is why having markers of success is an extremely effective strategy for seducing women. Women are influenced by the prevalent views of popular culture. And that prevalent view in popular culture is that success is "god". Dress like you are a successful man. Behave as if you shit gold. Act like you've got all of your shit together 100%.

Everyone doesn't know what the fuck is going on in this revolving earth that they suddenly found themselves in. For all we know, there could be a nuclear war in the next hour and we will all be dead. Yet, those who have learned to feign extreme confidence and act as if they've got it all together have been able to achieve far more success and generate more results than the rational "life is doom and gloom" losers. Positivity attract success.

SUBJECTIVE BIAS

It's a mistake to take a woman's words as the final truth because a woman doesn't see the world as it is; a woman sees the world as she is. A woman's own personal bias means that she has a subjective interpretation of reality - not an objective interpretation of reality. It would be foolish to take a woman's words as more than just clues about what the actual reality is. BE YOUR OWN SOURCE OF REFERENCE; DRAW THE TRUTH FROM WITHIN. In other words, have your own fucking opinion. Being a Yes Man and outsourcing your thinking to a woman is absolutely pathetic behavior.

EGO PROTECTION

A woman has a significant need to feel important. Women crave validation and approval from high status men for this very reason; it makes them feel valuable and fulfills a deep need for ego validation. A woman won't flat out say "I need to feel appreciated!" because this will make her look weak; instead she shows her need for approval with her behaviors. Even a "confident" woman craves your approval, attention and ego validation - even if she doesn't say this outright.

Understand the role of ego in communications is absolutely essential. A lot of what women say is just there to boost their own ego and feel important. When she talks its sometimes a matter of saying the kinds of things that will uplift her mood, and bolster her ego.

As a man, it's important that you have women work hard to win you over, and you have women jump through hoops on your behalf. Why? Because women value what they work for, and then to disregard that which is free and easily acquired. If a woman works hard to earn you, you better believe that she will appreciate you when she finally has earned you - much more than if you handed your heart and soul to her on a silver platter the moment you meet. WOMEN VALUE WHAT THEY WORK FOR is a maxim that you should burn into your mind, similar to the other maxims:

- (1) WOMEN VALUE MEN THAT VALUE THEMSELVES.
- (2) WOMEN MEN THAT OTHER WOMEN WANT.
- (3) WOMEN WILL VIEW YOU AS YOU VIEW YOURSELF.

Even if you "fell in love" with her the moment you saw her, don't let this be known and don't make grand confessions declaring your love. A woman is like a cat. Cats chase what is within their reach but not fully acquired; cats don't chase strings that they already have. You have play easy to be with, but hard to acquire. Don't give full validation because the full validation is exactly what keeps her chasing you. Use what you have as bait to keep women working hard for you (falling in love with you in the process); don't give away the bait for free.

It's imperative to understand that a woman has a deep need to feel important. Many of her actions stem from this basis of boosting her ego, and avoiding ego downfalls. For instance: a woman will buy expensive clothing she doesn't really need because it makes her feel valued and important. A woman won't make a move on a guy she likes because she is terrified of getting blown out and having her ego smitten. A woman is a slave to her ego - just like she is a slave to her personality. If you understand human nature, you'll be able to predict a woman's moves before they even happen - to an astonishingly shocking degree.

Men are very ego-centric. The right type of compliment can be very disarming and the start of a great mutually beneficial connection. That being said, understand that sucking up to men is detrimental - just like kissing a woman's ass is. No one respects the kiss ass; don't pedestalize mere mortals who were born - outside of their own choice - and will then one die with nothing. Even someone who is wealthy is unworthy of being worshipped; one day they will rot and perish from the earth that is not their own. Everything in this world is temporary. We are mere passerby making the most out of a bizarre situation of being born in a world that we didn't choose to be born in, and don't fully understand. Ultra successful people aren't inherently smarter or more talented than you. They just think differently. They just have different kinds of experience. They shouldn't be worshipped. Use them merely as case studies to learn from, and believe that you can surpass them. I pity the man who worships a woman just because she won a genetic lottery and was a born with a hole at the bottom of her body.

CONFIRMATION BIAS

A woman's tendency to only see evidence that supports her prior views of the world, and disregard contrary evidence that conflicts with her prior views of the world. Bait a woman to work hard towards winning you love. She'll then backwards rationalize her behaviors as evidence that she does indeed like you - solidifying her attraction for you. Further events will be interpreted as more evidence.

WOMEN'S BELIEFS FOLLOW THEIR BEHAVIORS

Before sex, a woman might have a 100 reasons why she doesn't want to sleep with you; however, after sex a woman will have a 100 reasons why you're worth sleeping with . A woman's line of reasoning simply follow their behaviors. She'll rationalize away everything she does to avoid feeling guilty; then continue to find evidence for her prior decisions and prior conclusions because of a confirmation bias. This is how people in cults stay in cults; they've invested so much into the cult that it would be heart-breaking for them to admit that their entire life was a lie, and that they are stupid as fuck for falling for the confirmation bias fallacy. My intention with this writing isn't to make women look like shit, but to teach you how they operate so that you can condition her mind to serve your dick.

LAW #88: BE GOOD AT TELLING YOUR STORY.

Story-telling is a vital aspect of communication. Have good stories.

He who controls the narrative, controls the relationship. Have the stronger frame. Be an effective story-teller and use stories to embed important values that you want her to internalize. Use stories that are emotionally relevant, integrate trending buzz-words, and a woman's personal trance words. Stories are incredibly effective tools of persuasion - even more so than logical lectures.

Know how to tell the most important story of all: your story. Be the master of that story. Spin it in a way that presents you in the best light.

LAW # 89: COMMUNICATE FROM A POSITION OF BENELOVENCE.

Don't hate women. It's simply a matter of understanding female nature and playing accordingly.

Female nature isn't inherently bad, or good. It just is - just like a snake won't be blamed for biting an ankle. The key is to use your understanding of female nature to your seductive advantage - NOT letting female nature use you. If you aren't a player of the game, then you are being played. STOP being a bystander. START PLAYING THE FIELD.

Don't hate the game. Don't hate the player. Just accept them for what they are, and play the game accordingly. Hating women unconsciously impacts your game by compromising your vibe. Women can sense inner-resentment[1], and will mirror it back (look up "Mirror Neurons" on Google for more info on that). It is more seductive to have a benevolent intent and leave women better than when you first found them.

~

1. Being bitter is a sign of a weak frame.

58

LAW # 90: SAY MORE WITH LESS WORDS.

Communicate more with less words.

Appear to be effortless and "mindless" - even if you're executing a well thought-out plan. Being spontaneous is disarming to women and puts them at ease. Women will often discuss sex as occurring in a manner that "just happened". A woman wants to "be swept in the moment" and fall into an enjoyable experience where "one thing led to another" ending in sexual pleasure. MEN JUST WANT THE END RESULT; women enjoy the process. While you're ready to fuck within minutes, a woman will want to be taken through an emotional rollercoaster ride that accumulates in sexual intimacy. Foreplay isn't just physical, but emotional, logistical and verbal.

He who tries hard, dies hard. Even if you're putting in a lot of effort into the interaction, appear to be effortless - like you're just going with the flow and riding the emotional waves.

Womenese is an art form. Take a moment to think about how you talk to girls.

- Do you always say what is expected of you?
- Are you speech patterns predictable?
- Do you say that which is safe?
- Are your conversations nice?
- Are you overly concerned with making women feel comfortable?

If you answered yes to 4/6+ more of these questions then you have a fucking problem, and that is that you're boring as fuck. If you learn anything from this book then let it be this incredibly important Womense concept: say more with less words.

59

LAW # 91: SEE THE WORLD FROM HER PERSPECTIVE.

When talking to a woman, make what you are saying RELEVANT to the core values that she believes in, and the core topics that she is interested in. Always relate it back to these things.

Talking from a position of situational relevance will ensure that your communications are SMOOTH and not weird. Be a wolf dressed in sheep clothing. Whatever you say to a woman, relate it back to what is emotionally valuable to her because a woman is always listening to the "What's in it for me?" Channel.

~

"Why do I need to learn to speak Womanese in order to understand Women? Why don't women just say what they mean and what they say? Why don't women just articulate clearly in their mind - instead of playing games?"

Reason #1: Women can very inarticulate. Even if a woman WANTS to accurately explain her perspectives she may be unable to do so because she is not good at putting her thoughts into words. Put simply: <u>**women suck at communicating effectively and instead just leave hints about what's on their mind.**</u>

Reason #2: Women will go to far lengths to avoid feeling socially awkward - even blatantly lying to your face. Women are physically more fragile than men and thus, since the caveman era: have used their social skills (instead of direct aggression) to gain power and exert influence. In other words, women will prefer to avoid awkward social confrontation if possible, and will use white lies to bend the truth to help them avoid these social confrontations. To a narcissistic female liar, lying is a way of life; the truth is simply a matter of how she feels like at that exact moment in time. A narcissistic female liar doesn't even feel guilty for lying because how desensitized she is to it; nor, would she even admit that her white lies are lies in the first place.

Reason #3: Women are not good at deciphering the truth themselves. A woman's strong emotions makes her susceptible to self-denial and self-deception. <u>**A woman is not in touch with the deeper side of her nature**</u>, and thus she can't say the truth even to herself. This is why asking women for dating advice is not prudent; her own intense emotional bias prevents her from assessing the situation in a clear light.

Reason #4: Certain dark truths are too ego-damaging, stigmatized and humiliating for a woman to confess to, so she'll lie to cover it up. The classic example of this is a woman's desire for sex. Women really do enjoy sex and crave it; however, they can't verbalize this explicitly because society (and religious men will judge them for it). If a woman is 18 and comes from a traditional family with spiritual values, she might be shamed by her social circle for engaging in "sinful lust". She doesn't want to feel slutty because the guilt is painful. So a woman with a traditional background will either deny her lust for men (even from herself and even if she engages in sex), or she will admit this lust for men for herself but will hide it from others - even as going as far saying that she is a "virgin". Women will easily bend the truth intentionally if they think it makes them look better; this is a woman's words can't be trusted and a man is forced to use tests/look for other indicators to ascertain the truth of the situation.

While you have purchased this book on womenese, understand that ultimately it doesn't matter what a woman really meant to say. What matters is TRUTH OF THE SITUATION. A woman meant to say something that would only have shed light to the truth of the situation, but not explained it entirely; its up to your detection skills to be able to use to clues to put together a puzzle piece that shows an accurate map of the reality.

LAW # 92: DON'T GET SUCKED INTO HER WORLD.

Don't spend too much time trying to figure a woman out. Pedestalizing a woman in your mind, leads to pedestalizing her with your behaviors. Ask yourself this question: "While I am spending my time thinking about her, is she spending time thinking about me?"

Don't get carried away thinking about a particular woman because thinking too much about a woman leads to developing oneitis and strong feelings - which then leads to needy behavior. The more you think about her, the more emotionally invested you become in her - eventually developing feelings for her. Instead of obsessively thinking about a particular woman (causing yourself to fall deeper into clutches) bait her to think about you by sending mixed signals.

Focus on sharpening your game skills - instead of getting a specific woman. You're learning game NOT to get a specific woman in general but to be good with women in general.

LAW # 93: FUCK OR BOUNCE.

Change her mind, change her experience.

HOW SHE SEES THE WORLD IS HOW SHE WILL EXPERIENCE IT. A positive outlook leads to a positive emotional experience. Hence, it is helpful to be positive when dealing with women to encourage them to focus on what's about good in life, and to experience the good emotions that comes from gratitude.

FUCK, OR BOUNCE. Don't be the friend.

NEWSFLASH: If you are knee-deep in the friend-zone with a particular woman then you're giving away the relationship benefits of being with you for free. You are giving away the best parts of yourself FOR FREE. It's much smarter to have a "cost" of being with you, and that "cost" is that women within your inner-circle need to "pay" is sexual access to their bodies - as well as an acceptance of specific frames that are conducive to that sex continuing to occur. These frames include accepting you as "THE AUTHORITY" in the dynamic between you and her, accepting your role as the leader who makes decisions for the both of you, and accepting you as THE PRIZE.

She "takes one for the team" by submitting to overtly sexual frames that you set up, and blatant physical advances - even if she isn't in the mood for sex right now. That being said, if you're good at touching a woman's body in specific areas (and using a correct sequence of motions), then she will WANT to have sex with you; she will become physically addicted to you, hooked on the chemicals released in her brain that come with your physical touch, and the pleasurable habits will overtake her. Women WANT TO HAVE SEX - just not with fucking socially-inept losers living in their mom's basement playing video-games all day long lacking in any cool hobbies/passions. BE THE APEX ALPHA WARRIOR.

It's essential for you to understand that YOUR TIME IS WORTH REAL MONEY. Your psychological energy is WORTH REAL MONEY. Are you giving it away FOR FREE to a woman who won't even reciprocate by allowing sexual advances to occur, and to allow the interaction progress at a reasonable pace towards sex? Well STOP.

A high status man wouldn't waste his time on bullshit, and women intuitively know this. They quickly lose respect for a man who puts up with bullshit.

You have enough friends in your life right now as it is, and you don't need more. You have to be clear about what you want out of her. Fuzzy goals lead to fuzzy results. Be willing to admit that you desire "dirty" sex with her; acknowledge this and then make moves to realize this goal. Continually progress the inter-action towards sex; increase the level of physical intimacy at a reasonable pace until you BANG THE SHIT OUT OF HER. Making a move will force a woman to show you the cards that she is holding; if she keeps putting ON the breaks then it's time to kick her to the curb and stop wasting your time.

Kicking her to the curb means letting go of the illusions

that you have developed in your mind that she is somehow "one of a kind" and "special". You need to BREAK YOURSELF - in regards to that false deception. She is NOT special. She is NOT one of a kind. She is NOT a unique goddess. These inaccurate perceptions are your feelings tricking you into mating; it's this psychological and emotional bonding process that has ensured the survival of the human race. You have to snap out of it and stop clinging on to the time-wasting narrative "that one day you will get her".

Don't you get it? If you're sinking in your time with a female friend that doesn't value you enough to see you in a sexual light then you are WASTING TIME that you could have spent on a woman who would value you in a sexual light, finding one that would, or developing your skills to have a higher level of worth in the sexual marketplace. OPEN YOUR EYES TO THE TRUTH: If you are too pussy to make a move on a woman that you like the you are pathetic. Your ancestors fought in WW1-WW2 - risking their lives in the battle-field - and you can't even show sexual intent? Yes, that's a fucking problem. And yes, you need to MAN THE FUCK UP SON!!! THIS MEANS YOU. THIS MEANS TODAY. THIS MEANS NOW.

Women are much smarter and more cunning than you realize. In fact, the average women is superior to a man in understanding dynamics in game. While men are busy talking about sports, video-games, working out and making money, women love gossiping and discussing relationships.They'll spend hours upon hours chatting over the phones over different issues encountered in man-to-woman interactions/relationships. This is why a lot of old-school set of memorized lines (known as routines) are centered around stories of couples; it's because next to cold reads, relationships are the second biggest chick crack subject. All of this talk about relationships has led to women having an acute understanding of the subject matter, and you should never underestimate the level of a woman's cunning - even if she's operating on an unconscious strategies. Men conquer worlds; women conquer the conquerers of worlds.

Women know what they are doing: when they string men along with false hope that one day the guy might have sexual access to her body. They'll keep the guy hooked, so that he will continue to do free favors for her in the meantime. Women like two different types of guys: providers, and lovers. On one extreme is the APEX ALPHA LOVER who turns her WET, and the other extreme is a BETA SIMP PROVIDER. If you aren't the lover then you are by default: the provider, and she is stringing you along with false hope of sexuality in the super distant future that may never happen.

YOUR TIME IS YOUR MOST VALUABLE RESOURCE and you're going to throw it down the toilet (!) with a woman who is playing waiting games with you? HA! When a woman friend-zones you, what she is really saying is that she doesn't consider you to be high status enough to be sexually-worthy, but she'll still use your resources in the meantime. She wants you to orbit around her so she can continue to exploit your imaginary relationship and false idealization of her - brought on by unreciprocated feelings. In the meantime, she'll continue her search for a better guy.

Women continue their cock carousal with Apex Alphas until they start sensing that their looks are fading and they need to lock-down a wealthy provider before their sexual market value plummets. It's not the guy that she's attracted to but his wallet and her performance in bed will reflect this - as she'll rush the guy to cum, so she can move on with her life. Women are not attracted to beta simp providers, but will still spend time with them for the sake of pragmatic purposes. Don't get bitter; GET BETTER.

<u>The first thing you can do to instantly raise your sexual market value is to get better at being a producer of emotions</u>

that women value - specifically fun, intrigue, and good emotions. Learn to generate these emotions from scratch with specific techniques that I mention in my first masterpiece book "Conversation Casanova Mastery". When you give tons of value (NOT the financial kind), you become valuable and eventually she becomes emotionally addicted to you.

You aren't asking the right questions. You are only asking "How do I please her?" instead of focusing on "How can she please me?" Alpha Males TAKE WHAT THEY WANT. TAKE VALUE by touching her body from the very start of the interaction, keeping the touching frequency, and escalating the level of intimacy in the touching. TAKE ACTION EVERY DAY MOTHERFUCKER!!!!

When a woman says "I need space" what she really means is that she needs your dick to move further away from her, so that another dick can enter inside. If you're taking up her time, then she has less time to invest in men perceived to be of higher worth in her eyes. Understand this Red Pill Truth about Women: A WOMAN WILL ALWAYS GO FOR THE BEST POSSIBLE OPTION AVAILABLE TO HER.

A woman's level of sexuality depends on the guy that she is with. An Apex Alpha male - running unconscious lover game - unleashes a woman's wild sexual side. The woman will behave like a sexual ANIMAL - enough to make a nice guy blush. A Wimpy Beta Male - who judges women negatively on their promiscuous nature, and runs predictable provider game - gets a woman's starfish position (if he even gets sex at all). When it comes to Beta Males women just stick around for pragmatic purposes such as resource extraction - rather than a lust for the guy's physicality and a genuine attraction to his personality.

The relevant Red Pill Truth here is: **ALPHA FUCKS, BETA**

BUCKS. Alphas get lustful sex with women because women are with them due to their personality and physicality; in contrast, betas get starfish sex with women (if any sex at all) because women are with them due to their financial resources and other practical purposes. Not every woman marries for love; some women marry for practicality.

What is considered "disgusting" versus "dangerously SEXY" depends on a man's level of attractiveness. A man who is clearly high in sexual market value is perceived as "cute" and his advances will be "cute; the same advances by a man who is low in sexual market value is perceived as "creepy" and "verbal harassment".

62

LAW #94: BYPASS EMOTIONAL BIAS. EXECUTE COLDLY.

As a man, learn to ignore your feelings and trust the evidence.

U nderstand this about how women understand the reality of the situation: A WOMAN WILL SEE THINGS ACCORDING TO WHAT GIVES THEM THE GREATEST EMOTIONAL PAYOFF. For instance: if a woman breaks up with a former lover then it gives her greater emotional payoff to say things like "I broke up with him because he was an asshole and a loser!! He had no future!" This gives her a greater emotional-payoff than to say something along the lines of "If everyone who I date is an asshole then maybe I am the asshole. There's something about me that makes men do crazy things that are against their best interest. I seem to feed off the attention that I get from generating drama and some men don't have time to deal with this pettiness. The guy is a pretty good guy, but he lacked the composure to deal with the nuclear shit-tests that I threw his way when I lost self-control and threw one of my classical temper tantrums."

Further, a woman's susceptibility to confirmation bias only

confirms her prior world views; in other words, women see the world as they are - not as the world actually is. This is why how a woman describes her friends and other people in her life reveals a lot about her personality. You can tell a lot about a woman about how she describes her prior associates. If she describes her prior associates in negative terms then be aware that you are dealing with a hypersensitive woman with poor conflict management skills and will generate negative vibes the second something goes wrong; however, if she describes her prior associates in positive terms then you'll know that she prioritizes positive vibes, and has good conflict management skills. Not all good fucks are good long term relationship material; when it comes to long term relationships, or the type of woman you would like to build a family with, there's a wide range of competency found in women and a woman's words provide a glimpse into her skill level of dealing with inherent challenges common in long term relationships.

Women are often too busy pursuing instant gratification and meaningless distractions such as the latest hype on Netflix, to invest time in figuring themselves out, and creating a realistic mature perspective in the reality that they live in; this is why women's perspective on life has a lot of inaccuracies, and why your masculine frame is the more competent one and should also be the dominant one in the relationship.

Remember: a submissive woman is a sexual woman; as a man, you should lead from the very start. By behaving like a dominant masculine man, you'll unleash her submissive feminine side and thus her sexual side.

63

LAW # 95: LISTEN TO UNDERSTAND - NOT JUST TO REPLY.

Use a woman's personal language, valued beliefs, and worldview when communicating with her.

"So what's the point of deciphering what a woman means to say and her view of the world?" the aspiring seducer ponders. The point is that it will allow you to speak to her in a way that is in her Personal Language. You want to answer a woman based on HER perspective of the world because this will resonate the most with her - rather than talking to a woman based on YOUR (more accurate) perspective of the world which will fall on deaf ears.

Let's say that you are suddenly teleported to Planet Homogobins. You're surrounded by green aliens with lizards living on their heads and long earrings that touch the ground. In this planet, these aliens stay awake from 12am-4am and spend the rest of the day deeply staring into the cosmos. These aliens speak in a different language than you, have different values, dress differently, and have an entirely different way of living (culture).

Normally you would do your own thing and give zero fucks

about green aliens and their irrelevant bullshit. You're too busy pursuing your own goals than to care about what green aliens care about. However, in this particular situation you realize that: (1) you need food to survive, and (2) you're horny as fuck and want to fuck green aliens that are legal. Therefore, you have to figure out (1) what is considered valuable on this planet so that you can trade it for food, and (2) what is considered to be high sexual market value and high social status in this culture, so that you can become that type of person.

The problem is that if you speak English to them, they won't even understand what you're saying. You need to learn a different language (Alien Womenese) to be able to communicate with them, and to be able to understand what they are saying/the signals they are sending out. Then in the process of reciprocal communication, you discover what is valuable to these green aliens on the planet and how you can give that sort of value as a form of currency in exchange for food. Then you discover the type of man that these green 18 year old female aliens find attractive and become that type of man - which (you guessed it) is communicated to you and you are able to learn, because you understand Alien Womense.

Women are not always aligned with their true nature. To ask a woman point-blank what do you find attractive in a man can lead to misleading answers. To figure out what a woman is actually attracted to, you have to look at THE TYPE OF MEN THAT SHE HAS HAD RELATIONSHIPS WITH IN THE PAST, WHAT SHE TALKS ABOUT, and HER BODY LANGUAGE RESPONSES. These are clues about which sort of behaviors and embodiment of traits will turn her on.

Each women has several (or one) sexy stereotype that she is attracted to - whether it's successful business man, spiritual guru, Bad Boy Rebel, The Party Guy, or corporate lawyer who fucks. Once you figure out which sexy stereotype is best aligned with your personality and the type of girl that you want to fuck, then the next step is to hang out in places where women are attracted to that type of guy. Develop a social circle and become the number one guy in that social circle because women fuck the APEX ALPHA MALE - not the #2. In the game of seduction, it's winner TAKES ALL and losers TAKE NOTHING. You have to be AT THE APEX.

KEY POINTS TO REMEMBER FROM PRIOR CHAPTERS:

- Don't just see what she said - look at what was NOT said.
- Don't just view what her words mean on the surface level; look for a deeper meaning.
- Much of what women do say is just random nonsense that isn't worth deciphering, but sometimes there are noteworthy remarks that will leave clues on how to seduce her - if you pay attention.
- Be a good detecting at deciphering the truth.
- Operate on a map of reality - instead of a map of illusions and self-denial.
- Listen to understand - not just to reply.

64

LAW # 96: BE AWARE OF YOUR AWARENESS.

You could be dealing with a female narcissist and not even know it!

Awareness is absolutely essential to protecting yourself from common exploitations used by aggressive women. If you thought women were stupid, think again; they often have a cunning agenda. This agenda can be so covert that even the manipulator may not be consciously aware of it. Even a woman's submission is a ruse to make you feel relaxed, let your guard down, and to gain your trust.

Men conquer worlds; women conquer men. Don't underestimate a woman's capacity for bullshitting you, and utilizing covert manipulation tactics for you to do her bidding.

How can you protect yourself from something that you don't even see!!?

Simply being aware of common female manipulation tactics will give you greater levels of immunity against them. Acute self-awareness = improvement.

When you become acutely conscious of covert manipulation tactics used by women then you'll be able to identify them in real-time when they occur, and STOP BEING AN EASY TARGET SUCKERED INTO THEIR TRAPS.

Here's the truth: female narcissists use people in the same manner that men use tools. The'll use the tool for all that it's worth and then discard it; cancel culture encourages women in hitting the "NEXT!!!" button and jumping on to a new dick the moment there is some conflict over a silly, petty issue.

When a psychopath is finished milking the cow until it bleeds, she will discard the target into the trash. She doesn't "love you" per se; she only "loves" what she gets out of you, and the idealization that you represent in her mind. If you are in a relationship with a narcissist, understand that they are with you for as long as they keep getting something out of you. The moment the value ceases to be available then they will disappear. Their "affection" is conditional.

Don't take it personally. It's just built into their nature. You wouldn't blame a wolf for eating a sheep; don't blame a predatory narcissist for going after someone she perceives as prey. It's important that you get what you want out of a relationship with a woman - just like she's ensuring that she's getting her needs met. THE FIRST KEY FOR DEALING WITH WOMEN IS TO KNOW WHAT YOU WANT. After all, if you aren't clear about what you want out of this whole connection then how do you expect to randomly get it?

The sense of loyalty that you feel is misguided. It isn't your responsibility to save her from herself, or to fix by playing the role of a therapist. Don't get attached because of your inner Savior Complex; playing the "Victim Card" is exactly what these narcissistic predators do to entrap you into their clutches and exploit you for psychological/emotional resources. Don't continue to drain time, energy, and money into a woman with emotional baggage and issues - hoping that she will magically change.

You would just waste months (sometimes years) of psychological energy trying to get a woman to change and still get barely move the bottom line forward. As a result, you'll miss out on other opportunities in the sexual marketplace. Realize that energy wasted on a sexual dead-end was vital energy you could have spent in developing yourself to reach your own full potential!

Female narcissists brainwash men into being servants, and these guys fall for it because:

- (1) they are desperate for some pussy,
- (2) they lack other options,
- (3) they don't have the game to generate new options,
- (4) they fail to recognize their tremendous potential, and
- (5) they have been brainwashed by society to pedestalize women with "the woman is always right" bullshit.

Getting into a sexual relationship with a beautiful woman at all costs - including selling out your soul - is not a "win". Don't sell out your life purpose and life goals just because you want some sex, and want the empty-ego-validation status of "lay+1" or "in a relationship". Making important life decisions with emotions and thinking with a dick has ruined the lives of many men.

BE A MAN ON YOUR LIFE PURPOSE. Have an amazing life. A woman is just a supplement to that. PUT YOURSELF

FIRST. Never compromise your life purpose or peace of mind for the sake of pussy; you'll lose self-respect, and she'll (unconsciously or consciously) lose respect for you too.

Narcissistic women are absolutely obsessed with themselves. They have difficulty seeing outside their own personal world. Empathy shown is fake. Altruism exuded is merely a ploy to gain your trust with virtue signaling before making a move for significant resource extraction.

If she's hanging around she's certainly getting something out of it. While every healthy relationship has a mutual exchange of value that is win/win, in the case of having a relationship with a toxic narcissist the relationship is often one-sided. There is a massive power-imbalance where one partner takes significantly more value than the other partner.

Men get trapped into one-sided imaginary relationships where they do all of the giving, and almost none of the taking. The woman tricks them into thinking that they just have to comply with their demands even more, so they can get access to a prior state of sexual access and physical intimacy. At this point, the man's feelings are so intense and he is so emotionally attached, that he continues to cling on to her and doing whatever she wants in the hopes of "winning" over her affection.

Unfortunately for him, she becomes disgusted with being worshipped in this matter and views his pedestalizations as proof that he is weak/inferior in the sexual marketplace. The more power he gives away by chasing her (without her reciprocating), the more disgusted she becomes; ironically, by trying harder to win her over, he actually loses her. Intuitively a woman knows that a high status man would LEAD and DOMINATE. A high-status man wouldn't beg, give up his social power, and make her the center of his life. By valuing yourself and putting yourself FIRST, women become more attracted to you.

Leveraged correctly, a woman can be a helper in helping

you achieve your life mission. Leveraged incorrectly, a woman can destroy you. Never underestimate the potential cruelty of women; their sexual nature is ruthless in easily discarding men perceived to be of low worth and trading up when the opportunity presents itself.

BE THE FUCKING BEST. When you're at the apex of the mountain, you don't have to worry about the competition. Be a predator. When you are skilled at manipulation tactics yourself, you'll be able to recognize when manipulation tactics are being used on you and properly counteract them. It takes game to recognize game. Learn the fucking rules of the game, and play them better than anyone.

65

LAW # 97: THINK AHEAD.

Always be a few steps ahead.

Womenese is the ability to understand female communication on a deep level, and being able to effectively communicate in a manner that is understood by females. Put simply: Womense is the art of being able to decode, and encode Female OS. When you can speak Womense fluently then you'll have ample insight into how a woman operates, and you'll able to predict her moves several moves in advance; when you know ahead of time how a woman will behave, you'll be able to have calculated moves ahead of time that preemptively disarm her. ALWAYS BE AT LEAST ONE STEP AHEAD OF HER.

And if you're really skilled at the game, you're several moves ahead of her - yet you come across as unscripted and in the present moment. No matter what a woman says, or does, you would have already anticipated it and have a prepared a counter-response.

One of the key strategies to effective game is to create a system designed to get you laid and sticking to that system every single day. By doing the same key behaviors over and over, you'll eventually get mastery over them. **After all, repetition is the mother of skill.**

- For instance, if you just have one opening line to start conversations with women and you focus on one area of meeting women then eventually you'll master both of them. You'll know the natural follow-ups that occur from that opening line. You'll know the nooks and crannies of that specific location (including the best specific times that women come out).
- In contrast, if you do something new each time then you won't actually master any thing. It's like someone who "trains" by trying 1 new instrument every week; the jack of all trades is the master of none, and it is mastery that gets you sexual results. Stick to one game-plan until it succeeds.

66

LAW # 98: STAY TRUE TO YOUR VALUES.

W hen you stand for nothing, you fall for anything. Don't compromise yourself.

THE DANGER OF SPEAKING WOMENSE

While this is a book that talks about learning to understand and speak Womense, there is an inherent danger that is worth mentioning, and that danger is being pulled too far into this blackhole of caring too much what women think. As an Alpha Male man, it is imperative that you have your own life purpose and goals that you're busy focusing on; don't take Womense too far and start obsessing with thoughts like:

- "What did she really mean when she said THAT?!"
- "How did she interpret my words?!"
- "How did she interpret my interoperation of her words?"
- "What was running through her mind when I responded this way to her?!"

- "What did I say that caused her to behave in THIS WAY?"
- How will I be perceived if I behave in this specific way?"

These thoughts are conducive to the Analysis Paralysis Trap, Excuseitis Trap and the Information Trap. These traps are incredibly common and they stop men dead in the tracks from succeeding with women. Highly intelligent men are especially susceptible to having their sharpened intellect work against them.

I. ANALYSIS PARALYSIS TRAP

In the Analysis Paralysis Trap, the man is too busy thinking about the situation to act. While The Thinker is busy thinking, the Man of Action runs laps around The Thinker. The key is to set a limit to how much time one spends in analyzing the situation, and then when that limit is reached: FOCUS ON RAW, PURE ACTION IN THE FIELD.

II. EXECUSEITIS TRAP

In The Excuseitis Trap the aspiring seducer uses his high IQ to come up with different reasons why today is not a good day to take action - landing from "I'm too old and unattractive" to "She probably has a boyfriend." As soon as one allows for excuses then he will easily become frozen because there is always a "VERY LEGITIMATE" excuse readily available to avoid taking action. The higher the IQ one is, the smarter and more sophisticated the excuses will sound. The key is to take it upon yourself to have a "NO EXCUSES ALLOWED POLICY!!!"

III. THE INFORMATION TRAP

Finally in the Information Trap, the aspiring seducer doesn't take action because he perceives himself having a lack of necessary information; he's fallen into the mistaken belief of "I can't do anything, until I know everything." The aspiring seducer mistakenly tries to come up with a PERFECT PLAN based on ALL OF THE INFORMATION and then take PERFECT ACTION. The problem with this is that there is such thing as the perfect pickup. Pickup is messy. In the process of seducing women, mistakes will be made, and that's okay. The key is to keep going with confidence and hold a confident frame of "It's ALWAYS ON. Everything is going according to plan."

DON'T GROW A VAGINA. Spending a little bit of time seeing the world from a woman's perspective does have its practical uses. See the world from a woman's eyes, and you'll be able to better understand her needs, AND how her needs and your needs aligned - creating a win/win connection with the beautiful woman (a mutually beneficial exchange of value). However, spend too much time seeing the world from a woman's eyes, and you'll start losing your own identity and sense of personal priorities.

Spend too much time trying to understand how a woman thinks, and you'll develop a vagina; while a little of a good thing is beneficial, too much of it is harmful. Just because you're reading a book to understand how women THINK, doesn't mean you should spend all of your time pondering how women think because that would result in you becoming feminine and pedestalizing pussy. Spend a bit of time each day researching seduction-self-help topics, but don't spend more than an hour on the subject matter; it's better to prioritize taking action in the field and reaching your full potential than delving deeper into research. FOCUS ON YOUR PERSONAL DEVELOPMENT.

Remember that one of the primary Alpha Male Rules of Life is: PUT YOURSELF FIRST. Women are too busy obsessing over themselves to care too much about you. If you don't care about yourself then you will be lost. YOU HAVE TO BE A FIGHTER FOR YOURSELF! That's a job no one can do but you! Take care of yourself just like you would take of a best friend; push yourself just like a coach would push a client.

SEE A WOMAN'S WORLD, BUT DON'T GET SUCKED INTO IT You'll notice that women will often embellish details in their narratives because they would rather live in an imaginary, pleasant fantasy than confront a harsh, painful reality. Spending too much time thinking about what a woman is thinking is a waste of psychological energy because the opportunity costs are significant. You spent so much time thinking about a particular woman ("What did she mean when she did THAT? What was the deeper meaning behind what she said that day?") that you failed to develop yourself further and failed to pursue other women. When one's emotions become engaged it can be VERY EASY to spend hours replaying scenes in your mind thinking about what it all means, instead of focusing on high priority tasks and your life's purpose.

Further, women's inner-worlds are not built on objective truth but rather pleasant lies. When you discover the deep truths about how women understand the world, you'll also get the rude awakening that women's perspective on the world is pathetic, inaccurate and dark. While it is beneficial for your sake to understand what women VALUE, so you can deliver that form of value to them and BECOME VALUABLE, it's also important to not be too pulled into a woman's frame. While it's beneficial for your sake to having a working knowledge of how women view the world, so you can understand how they operate, don't be swept into their perspective and start behaving like a woman yourself; you want to look into the darkness, but not be pulled into it. HAVE THE STRONGER FRAME. Even if a woman's frame is incredibly strong, your frame must be even stronger!!!

There is an extremely important concept to understand: PSYCHOLOGICAL IMMUNITY. Women exploit mentally-weak men for their resources. If a woman recognizes that a man with money is mentally weak then she will put her hooks on him; she'll send sexy photos, use endearing language like "babe", and make (empty) "promises" to snare him into his world. Once the man becomes emotionally and psychologically addicted to her pussy, she'll suddenly withdraw her attention, affection and access to her pussy. The man will then do whatever she wants to get back what he became used to.

WHEN A MAN STANDS FOR NOTHING, HE FALLS FOR ANYTHING. When a man in a relationship doesn't have a life purpose, and life goals: then a woman easily takes over his life, and her frame becomes his frame. Her thoughts and values becomes his thoughts and values. He loses his own identity and becomes just like her - turning her into the center of his universe. The man grows a vagina. Women find this simp type of behavior incredibly repulsive.

WHEN A MAN STANDS FOR SOMETHING, HE HAS PSYCHOLOGICAL IMMUNITY. As a man, it's important to have your own goals, and life purpose that you are striving for every single day. Make each day count! It has been said in the seduction community: "The best way to get women is to have something better to do than to get women." Women can sense when a man has nothing going on his life, and its very unattractive.

In contrast, when a man has an exciting lifestyle and an exciting life mission then the woman gets swept into his world. She accepts the man's thoughts and perspectives as her own. She changes her personality to help the man on his life's mission. This is where you want to be. BE A DECISIVE WARRIOR who inspires followers,

Women want to follow and submit to a more dominant man, but they won't follow a loser who can't get his shit together. Get your shit together. Become a leader. And watch women follow your lead - psychologically, logistically, and of course most importantly: physically. Dominate completely. Own her soul.

67

SPECIFIC EXAMPLES

WHAT SHE SAYS VERSUS WHAT IS REALLY HAPPENING

CHECKING OUT YOUR AVAILABILITY

- 1 "Do you have a girlfriend?"
- 2 "Are you Single?"
- 3 "Is anyone home with you?"
- 4 "I'm sure your girlfriend would enjoy that." [Or mentions your girlfriend at all] to bait you into saying "I don't have a girlfriend".
- 5 "Are you seeing anyone?"

She is assessing your level of social proof, and your availability in the sexual marketplace. This can be because she interested in you for her personal self, or potentially she wants to hook you up with a female friend that has in mind.

Assuming that this is a serious question and not a sarcastic question (based on her body-language) respond by mentioning that you had a prior ex-fiancé in the very distant past, but you're single in the present. While you do have "female friends", you are still searching for "the right one".

BINGO ◊ If a woman is asking these type of questions (in combination with positive body-language) then it's a strong sign that she interested in you.

◊ CHECKING OUT YOUR LEVEL OF INVESTMENT

- 6 "Do you love me?"
- 7 "Did you miss me?"
- 8 "To what extent do you love me?"
- 9 "Is she more pretty than I am?"
- 10 "Are you free now?"

She is setting you up to be susceptible to a big ask. By saying that you love her, it will naturally follow that you'll agree to do whatever she asks afterwards. Women want loyal soldiers in their army. These questions are designed to see if you're a loyal soldier in her personal army, and thus how much she can take from you.

She wants to see how much power she holds over you, so that she can unconsciously decide how much bullshit she can get away with in the future. She is going to do some stupid shit, and have you put up with because of your "love".

This is a cocky question because it assumes that you're already in love with her. It lets you know that you may be dealing with an overly arrogant woman who assumes that she has more worth in the sexual marketplace than she actually does.

These type of questions could also mean that she is feeling insecure and wants to get some quick ego validation by affirming that at least she has you in her life. It's important to look at the context to properly interpret her words.

Keep in mind that a woman who is feeling insecure is easier to seduce than a woman who is arrogant. Combine giving a compliment with physical escalation at the same time; say "You have sexy legs" as you massage her leg. Verbally framing the interaction as having a sexual charge sets the stage for further smooth physical escalation.

◌ FISHING FOR COMPLIMENTS

- 12 "I'm so fat."
- 13 "I'm so ugly."
- 14 "This dress doesn't look good on me."
- 15 "You don't even like me."
- 16 *flashes a part of her body to you*

The woman is feeling insecure, and wants you to validate her ego by correcting her. When she says that she's fat, she wants you to confirm that she is still attractive. When she says she is ugly, she wants you to tell her that she is pretty.

When she flashes a part of her body to you "accidentally", it's because she wants you to physically escalate on her.

◌ PLAYING BUILD A BETTER BETA

- 17 "We aren't communicating that well."
- 18 "We need to talk."
- 19 "You should do [xyz]."
- 20 "You should stop doing [abc]."
- 21 "You should apologize to me."

What she means to say is *"You aren't listening to me me explain why my needs are important."* In these instances, the women wants to continue the relationship and is working towards building you into the type of person that she thinks she is more compatible with in the long term.

Unfortunately, often women don't give good advice when they tell you to behave a specific way. They'll tell you who they think they are attracted to, but they actually aren't attracted to the ultimate nice guy that they're preaching you to become. Remember: when seeking advice on how to catch fish, ask a fisherman - not a fish.

ATTEMPTING TO PUT YOU INTO THE FRIENDZONE

- 22 "I don't want to ruin our friendship."
- 23 "I see you as just a friend."
- 24 "I'm not going to have sex with you."
- 25 "I'm going to go to your place, but we're not having sex."
- 26 "I thought we weren't going to have sex!"
- 27 "We shouldn't be doing this."

When a woman mentions the fact that she wants you to only be friends with her then this is because she isn't attracted to you in the moment, and **sees your genes as inferior.** Keep in mind that for men attraction is a light-bulb switch, but for women **attraction is a volume knob.**

While it is true that she doesn't feel attraction for you right now at this exact moment which is why she says some bullshit like "we are not going to have sex!", it is also true that women live in the emotions of the moment and her feelings about you can change.

She might mean what she is saying at that exact moment,

but the situation can change and she can suddenly become sexually aroused later. The appropriate response to these kind of statements is to explain to the female is "We'll see. I'm quite charming."

⬭ THE MOST CUNNING GAME THAT WOMEN PLAY IS PRETENDING THAT THEY AREN'T PLAYING ANY GAMES

- 28" I want honesty. Don't play any games."
- 29 "I hate games."
- 30 "Tell me the truth."
- 31 "You know you can tell me anything, right?"
- 32 "I won't judge you. Just spill the beans."

What a woman really means when she says these things is *"I want to see the cards that you're holding, so that I can better manipulate you."* A woman is a player of the game, but she'll pretend that she isn't playing any games - sometimes even to herself - to disarm you into revealing all of the cards that you are holding.

Here is the truth: women appreciate challenge. It excites them. The moment you confess your full love to her is the moment that her pussy dries up because it means that she will be bored out of her mind, and she'll seek to chase someone else. Confessing your feelings might make you feel better because you experience catharsis, but it removes the exciting challenge and thrill of the chase that women want to experience.

A woman isn't control of herself enough to be above human nature. It's within human nature to value things that are scarce and hard to get more than things that are overly available and easy to get. This is why it's important to not give a woman full disclosure. **A bit of mystery keeps her thinking**

about you. You wouldn't watch a movie if you knew the ending because it is the not-knowing that keeps you hooked.

⬤ HERE COME THE EXCUSES TO PULL THE WOOL OVER YOUR EYES

- 33 "I'm busy right now with my career."
- 34 "I have homework to do."
- 35 "My cat can't be alone right now."
- 36 "I'm in the middle of an emergency."
- 37 "It's late and I have to go to sleep."

If a woman uses her career as an excuse then what she is really saying *"My career is more important and fun than you. This is true even though my career is boring and tedious."*

Here is the truth about excuses: **when there is a will, there is a way.** This bears repeating: **WHEN THERE IS A WILL, THERE IS WAY.**

When a woman wants to spend time with you then SHE WILL MAKE TIME FOR YOU - even if she is busy. She will find a way to make it happen.

- She'll cancel her other plans.
- She'll say "no" to other people, so that she can make time for you.
- She'll reschedule at at time when she's available.
- She'll do certain things faster, so time can be made.

No one really has time for anything. Time is "created" by being planned for. Inquire about her schedule and then give her a specific meetup time to meet up with her.

In contrast, if she isn't interested in you then she'll find lots of excuses to let you down easily - without hurting your feelings. The excuses are just there to avoid bruising your ego. The truth is that if she keeps giving you excuses, she is really saying that there are lots of things that have a greater priority than you.

A woman's availability (or lack of) shows how much she is sexually interested in you. If she seems to always be busy, without a very strong good reason, and she doesn't suggest other times to meet-up then she just ins't interested in you. In contrast, if she suggests other times to meet up, then she is interested in you. It's important to gauge a woman's interest level in you to filter out women who are too low interest to be worth your time.

💧 THE FAKE YES

- 38 "Fine."
- 39 "K" (in texting)
- 40 "Do what you want."
- 41 "Whatever."
- 42 "You can do whatever you want because I don't care!"

These statements in the context of a relationship are actually quite misleading. On one hand, she is saying that you can do what you want, but on the other hand she is doing it in a bitter way. What does she really mean?

What she really means to say is *"I'll pretend to not care for my ego, but I'll extract vengeance later by being passive aggressive and emotionally abusive."* In other words, **SHE DOES CARE** (based on the fact that she said what she said in a butt-hurt type of way), but she is pretending that she doesn't care in order to feed her ego the message *"I am important. I don't need anything from anyone."* It hurts a woman's ego to admit that she needs something, and to admit that she cares, so she pretends that she doesn't.

THE FAVOR DIGGER

- 43 "Lets build a bookshelf."

What she really means to say is *"You do the work. I'll help out by watching and giving suggestions."*

- 44 "This thing that I have to do is very hard."

She wants to bait you into helping her, but her ego is too fragile to admit that she can use your help. If you try to help her, she could say "no" (even though she wants you to help her) so that she doesn't feel like she is imposing a burden on you.

THE PLEASE CHANGE THE SUBJECT CRY FOR HELP

- 45 "Uh huh"

I don't really care about what you just said, but I'm trying to be polite so I'll respond with a one-word. Please change the subject to something is more aligned to my core values.

- 46 *one worded response*
- 47 *(in person body-language) looks in the other direction while you're talking to her*

I don't really care about what you said, but I have to be nice, so I'll say something.

- 48 On FB gives you a thumbs up   response to your long message (or she takes a really long time to respond to your message)

I don't care about what you just said and the topic that you just brought up is boring, but I don't want to look like a bitch and completely severe our connection, so here is a droplet of ego validation.

68

MORE SPECIFIC EXAMPLES

4 **9 "I want a stable future"**
I want you to pay for everything, while I relax at home.
50 "You won't understand."
I don't even understand it, so I can't explain it to anyone.
51 "Why did you break up with your last ex girlfriend?"
Do you have any serious problems that I should be concerned about?
52 "This guy asked me out today."
I want to make you jealous, so you would finally ask me out already.
53 "What do you think of Jenny?"
Is she someone who I should be concerned about? Is there competition that I should be worried about? Are you going to badmouth her and thus badmouth me too?
54 "Come here."
55 "Hold this for me."
"Help me with this homework."
I want to see if you're a little bitch who will do whatever I want like a little doggie.
56 Mentions her ex-boyfriend

I am still in love with him. I'll tell you that he doesn't mean anything to me, but the truth is that he means the world to me.

57 "You're cool and I like you, but..."

She doesn't really like you, but she's bringing the compliments to avoid hurting your feelings. Notice the "but" which is a way of retracting the prior statement.

58 "I am not upset."

She is upset but she is saying that she is NOT upset to calm herself down, and avoid losing her temper.

59 "I don't want to talk about it."

I don't have enough evidence to bring a compelling argument yet. **OR** *I want you to figure out why I'm upset by yourself.*

60 "I am very caring."

I am controlling. I use my "caring" as a guise to get what I want.

61" I want to be friends first."

You don't turn me ON. If you were hot then i would be all over you.

62 "I'm open-minded and non-judgmental."

I am desperate. I use these politically correct words to disguise my neediness.

63 "I'm outgoing."

I will talk your ear off. I'm LOUD..

64 "Are you gay?"

Why haven't you made a move on me already? I desire to feel desired.

65 "I'm not looking for a relationship right now."

I am not looking for a relationship with you.

66 "You're just like a brother to me."

In my eyes, you're a sexual dud.

67 "I like adventure and meeting new people"

I'm telling you now that I'm promiscuous, so as to soften the blow and so you won't come raging at me later

68 "You should enjoy the pleasures of life."

She's into you, and hinting that you show become more passionate towards her.

69 "The guy thought you were hot."

I think you're hot, and I'm projecting my own perspective on to the situation.

70 "I don't remember the price."

It's expensive, and I don't want to tell you because I'm trying to being the bringer of negative emotions.

71 "I want new furniture."

I want a complete home reconstruction. I'll just be starting with this, but as time goes on: I'll have a lot more things on the list.

72 "It's a girl's night out."

Tonight I will do whatever I want. I'm creating the justification for it now, so as I can use that as a defense "I already told you that it's a girl's night out) in the case that you try to use it against me. I'm also justifying it for myself now, so I don't feel guilty later about all the stupid shit that I'm going to do.

73 "Did you get a chance to do the thing I asked about?"

Hey!!! GET IT DONE!!! I mean now!

74 "Sure, I don't mind paying."

Yes, I do mind. But I'll say that I don't mind, so that I can avoid feeling like a bitch. Secretly, I wish you will insist.

75 "Now is not a good time."

I have other priorities which are more important than you.

76 "You give me your number."

I'm not planning on calling you, but I want to avoid an uncomfortable confrontation; therefore, I'm going to use a socially acceptable white lie and imply that I'll call you even though I won't.

77 "I'm upset."

This one means exactly what she said.

78 "I'm not going to have sex with you."

I am not going to have sex with your right now, but maybe later if I get TURNED ON.

79 "Am I fat?"

I am baiting for compliments. Tell me I'm pretty, so I can feel better about myself.

80 "We need to talk; don't get mad."

I'm just saying that to avoid triggering you when I bring out the "big guns". I'm going to use that conversation as a way to complain.

81 "I need to think about it."

I'll just say that to avoid looking like a bitch, but if I had balls like a man then I would be direct and just say NO.

82 "I feel like I've known you forever."

I really like you.

83 "You never listen!!"

You listen sometimes but at this moment, I feel like you never listen. I'm just saying what I FEEL like the truth is.

GOLD DIGGING QUESTIONS

- **84 "What job do you have?"**
- **85 "Are you in college?"**
- **86 "Hey, is this your car?"**

I'm curious to your potential as a provider.

87 "What are you doing this weekend?"

She wants you to ask her out.

88 "Tell me about yourself."

Tell me things about yourself that showcase what makes you attractive.

69

DEEPER EXPLAINATIONS

"Do you have a girlfriend?"

S he is assessing:

- your level of social proof,
- your availability in the sexual marketplace, and
- your level of confidence.

Assuming that this is a serious question, and not a sarcastic one (you'll be able to tell based on her body-language, the amount of interest that she has given you in the mutual past history) respond by mentioning that you had a prior ex-fiancé in the very distant past, but you're single in the present.

Bringing up an ex-fiancé will take away the "fuck boy" persona:

- get her drunk on your personality,
- fuck her in the pussy,
- take photos for underground FB groups and forums,

- discard like she is nothing but leftover trash,
- repeat cycle,
- lose your soul in the process of chasing temporal sensual pleasures,

but also signal that you're sexy enough for OTHER women to be interested in. Remember: women want a man that other women want. A high status man who doesn't have beautiful women as "friends" in his life and never had any prior lovers sets off unconscious Red Flags that there must be something wrong with him (he has no women in his life because he is fucking socially inept dork).

Saying that you are currently single will show her that you're AVAILABLE in the sexual marketplace. Further, if you have an ex-girlfriend just randomly show up around the house or at your work place, then this could be a significant annoying turn-off for other women.

In regards to these lessons that I am writing to you now: I paid for these lessons with incredible pain. I paid for them by going through fiery trial and error. Experience is one hell of a motherfucking teacher - absolutely brutal but effective. Become a lifelong student of the game of life and seduction; there's always more to learn, and a higher level of skill to achieve. One can't achieve perfection, but one CAN achieve an impressive level of competency to stay competitive in the sexual marketplace.

"Do you love me?"

In the context of a relationship: this could also mean that she's had a tough day at work, and is feeling insecure. Your words of validation will give her a boost of morale. She's implying that she has an emotional and psychological need to feel important and she wants you to fill that need with your words.

She is setting you up to be susceptible to a big ask. By saying that you love her, it will naturally follow that you'll agree to do whatever she asks afterwards. She's conditioning you to be a personal butler. These behaviors are relatively normal; it is human nature for one to go after what they want - especially for beautiful women who have become used to getting what they want from men since a young age.

It goes without saying that what a woman says at the pickup phase can have a different meaning than what she says at the relationship phase. Saying "Do you love me?" at the pickup phase would be a power-grab and a power-assessment. This is true even if it said with a smile and playfully to disguise its true intentions.

- -> Firstly, she wants an ego rush of knowing that she has a high-status man such as yourself, who is in love with her.
- -> Secondly, she's assessing how much power she has over you, and will then use that knowledge to gauge how much she can take from you. If she senses that you're really into her then she'll know that she has a lot of "social capital" and can take whatever the fuck she wants - making unreasonably large requests. If she senses that you're somewhat of a challenge, then she'll be on her best behavior to keep giving you value so that you'll stick around and allow her to keep extracting value.

Women won't necessarily admit this, but they appreciate challenge. They detest a man who is too easy to get. If a man is too easy to acquire, she'll assume that he lacks options. She intuitively expects a high-status man to have options.

Don't use the L word too early on in the connection, unless you want to get rid off her because you're sick of her bullshit.

Confessing your feelings to a woman too early will remove the level of challenge that makes her want to invest in you because why chase a string if you already have it?

This is why it is best to not give a woman full validation, so that she will be like a cat who keeps chasing string. Dread game (implying that you have options) will make a woman anxious enough to keep fighting to keep you.

Give a woman a specific compliment and observe her reaction. If she immediately responds with a conscious/unconscious signal of disinterest then this is a sign that she doesn't like compliments from men, and you should follow up with a tease 😈 to release the tension ("too bad you're such a dork"). As I mentioned multiple times in this book, a woman's body-language will betray the truth even if a woman will try to verbally disguise it because the truth always shines through. Ignore her words; look at what she does and the signals her body is sending out.

"To what extent do you love me?"

She is going to do some stupid shit, and have you put up with because of your "love". This question is similar to "Do you love me?" but it said with different words. The key is to understand that it is not the words verbatim that matters, but the idea behind the words. "To what extent do you love me" is the same as if she said "how much do you love me?"

"We aren't communicating that well."

You aren't listening to me me explain why my needs are important.

She really wanted to say "You are not communicating that well", but she is using the words "we" as a softener (so your feelings don't get hurt), and as an insidious method to get you to accept her idea as your own.

Women are naturally manipulative because they don't say the truth straight the way that it is. Don't take it personally. These women don't even know that they're being manipulative; they see it as a normal way of life. A fish born in water - spending a lifetime in water - doesn't even recognize there is such as a thing as "air".

The key here is not to be angry with women. Nor is to explain what they truly mean when they say all sorts of random bullshit. If you explain to a woman what the secret signals are that she is sending out then she'll become self-conscious and stop sending them out. Don't reveal your source of information, or it will become contaminated. Just acknowledge the reality and play the game accordingly.

There's a saying: "Don't hate the player. Hate the game." It's more accurately to say, don't hate both. Make peace with the dark reality of what works in the game, and what doesn't. Accept the world for what it is, and play accordingly. Respect the rules of nature.

"I don't want to ruin our friendship."

Your genes are inferior. Your personality and physicality don't turn me ON.

At this point, in the vast vast majority of cases you should make a move, and let the cards fall where they will because you have enough friends as it is.

"I want honesty. Don't play any games."

I want to see the cards that you're holding, so that I can better manipulate you. I want full disclosure and transparency because I want full control over you, and the resources that I can extract. In return, I may or may not engage in selective honesty.

A relationship is a hidden negotiation table. You bring something of value to the table, and she brings something of value to the table. There's a mutually beneficial exchange of value. You appreciate the value proposition that she has to offer, and it works the other way around too! She pickups up the contribution that you put down, and vice-versa.

If she wants full transparency and honesty in a relationship then expect her to the same, because this type of communication works both ways; if you're the one who is putting in all the effort and she is barely putting in any effort then you're in an "imaginary" one-sided relationship that is doomed to fail (because women only value what they work for).

The truth is that women don't want full disclosure because it makes you boring. Think of going to a movie that you already know the ending to. It would be incredibly boring to watch that movie because it's spoiled; there's no mystery, intrigue, or hidden surprises

70

SILENT COMMUNICATION

W omen are fickle creatures.

- You're spending time trying to understand them, when they don't even understand themselves. And when you can barely understand yourself.
- You expect women to keep their promises to you, when they don't even keep promises to themselves. Nor do you keep promises to yourself.
- You expect women to be honorable and not cheat with higher status men, when they often lack the self-control to keep themselves from eating a fattening chocolate donut. Women are not honorable; they are ruthlessly opportunistic.

Get your expectations straight.

- You expect to manage women, yet you barely can manage yourself.

- You expect women to be submissive, respect your decisions, and follow your lead, yet you haven't achieved much in your life and your competency is close to null - so who says you are worth following?
- You expect to be a Casanova with women, but you barely clock in one hour of practice a week?

Everything comes down to being the best option that a woman can choose at her given time. The cold truth is that a woman is inherently selfish. Her primary agenda is to serve herself. Being with you should be a clear win for her, just like it is a clear win for you.

The key to dealing with women is to convey the message that you are a lover by the behaviors that you do when you're around her. Treat her like a lover, and you'll create a romantic sexualized frame. Treat her like a friend, and don't be surprised that you're knee-deep in the friend zone. Understand that you are communicating messages to women simply by your choice of actions.

DON'T DO:

- #1) Behave like a man without a dick = friend-zone.
- #2) Hide your dick = friend-zone.
- #3) Never express any sexual interest = friend-zone.
- #4) Don't flirt with women = friend-zone.
- #5) Don't tease, touch, role-play, or use future-projections = friend-zone.
- #6) Never make a woman jealous by flirting with other beautiful women = friend-zone.
- #7) Appearing to be lonely and without close contacts = friendzone.

- #8) Believing that women are innocent angels who are disgusted by sex = friendzone.

DO:

- #9) Owning your dick and sexuality = lover-zone.
- #10) Whip out your dick = lover zone.
- #11) Conveying sexual intent = lover zone.
- #12) Being flirtatious = lover zone.
- #13) Using attraction amplifying tactics = lover zone.
- #14) Using the nuclear bomb of making a woman jealous = lover-zone.
- #15) Implying social proof and appearing popular = loverzone.
- #18) Understanding that women are sexual creatures who enjoy sex and desire to be desired = lover zone.

Your actions convey your belief system which then influences her belief system. What you do is a form of silent communication.

- For instance: if a woman calls you and you don't pickup the phone then you are silently communicating that you are a man of ambition, action and you have shit going on - thereby spiking your perceived worth through scarcity.
- In contrast, if you're always available then women will simply assume that you don't have a lot going on in your life; she's thinking "Why else is he available every day of the week for dates? Why else does he respond instantly whenever I reach out to him?" Women might not say this outright but they crave a man who has his own shit going on, and his

own life mission that he is focusing on. These are sexy traits that you are communicating indirectly by how you behave.

Don't always attach true meaning to what a woman says. She might not even understand what she just said and will forget about it later. <u>Constantly spending time figuring out what she means will put you into reaction mode. Live life in proactive mode - not in reactive mode.</u>

<u>Sometimes a woman will enter an intense emotional state and say some random bullshit that she doesn't mean in order to get emotions and thoughts out of her system - as a form of catharsis.</u> You don't need to waste valuable energy responding to what she just said. Ignore and misdirect to a different subject. OR you can deflect what she said with humor through the agree and amplify to absurdity technique. Just let her empty words pass through, and move on with your life.

<u>Understand that although a woman is an adult, she is still like a child on an emotional level.</u> While you are communicating to her mind, understand that you are simultaneously communicating to this inner-child.

This is why it's important to not be overly sensitive by pedestalizing her too high with too many compliments, supplications, begging, or excessively being defensive. If you treat a woman like a superior, she'll start viewing you as an inferior and become disgusted. WOMEN WANT TO BE WITH POWERFUL MEN. HENCE, YOU MUST SEIZE THE SOCIAL POWER IN INTERACTIONS.

- Don't talk badly about yourself - even in a self-deprecating humorous manner.
- Don't put her on a pedestal or she will look down on you.

- Don't talk negatively about your friends because that only comes to reflect negatively on you for spending time with those friends.

On the other side of this extreme, don't treat a woman too harshly. Women appreciate ego validation and attention from high status man. A WOMAN VALUES HER EGO MORE THAN SHE VALUES MONEY. Give respect to get respect; what you put into a relationship is what you will get out of it. That being said, keep mutual flirting ongoing to spike her excitement levels, and keep her emotionally engaged.

Being boring is the cardinal sin of dealing with women. Use an edgy, polarizing communication style and be a man of adventure to keep women hooked to being with you.

LAW # 99: TRUST FEMALE NATURE.

- **Don't trust so much what a woman says she will do.** Women say all sorts of random bullshit that they don't understand.
- **Don't trust a woman's sense of honor, and doing "what's right'.** Women are hardened to do that which feels the best in the given situation that they are in, and that which is the most advantageous to them.

TRUST FEMALE NATURE. Trust that a woman will do that which is within her nature to do because her capacity to exercise her freedom of will (to act against her nature) is very limited.

Don't think she is different.

LAW #100: A BULLETPROOF FRAME WILL CHANGE HER MIND.

A lot of guys fuck up because they don't have an independent mind. Their identity changes based on the woman who they are with. They turn into "Yes Men" who just agree with everything a woman says for the sake of rapport.

The truth is that women are sexually attracted to men who are leaders. Lead with competence, confidence - psychologically, physically and logistically.

A woman can have an intensely strong frame (conviction in her belief about reality and what the best plan of action in a situation is) but your frame should be EVEN STRONGER. You need to believe in yourself more than she believes in herself. By having extremely intense conviction and confidence in what you're doing, women end up falling into your frame, your world, and your dick.

Remember: the strongest frame wins.

CONCLUSION

KEY POINTS FROM THIS BOOK

1) Women make decisions and perceive the world through the medium of how they feel. By changing a woman's mood, you'll be able to change a woman's mind and behaviors. 🔑 <u>Control her emotions = control her perspective of the situation = control what she does.</u>

#2) A lot of guys try to communicate with women through logical persuasion which falls on deaf ears on women who are emotional creatures. You have to learn to press a woman's emotional buttons. 🔑 <u>Control her emotions = control her behaviors.</u>

#3) A lot of guys can't even manage their own emotions yet they expect to manage a woman's emotions. Mastery starts from within. By learning how to lead yourself, you'll learn how to lead other people - women and men included. 🔑 <u>By improving your own emotional state, you'll improve the emotional state of those around you.</u>

#4) Even the most dominant of women, wants to be dominated by a stronger and more competent man. Lead the men and the women will follow. Lead a woman and she'll get TURNED ON . Learn to be an effective leader by being competence, and leading with confidence. **STRONG DOMINANCE CONVEYS INTENSE CONFIDENCE.**

#5) What a woman says is not what she truly means because what she said was based on her current emotional state. As her current emotional state is subject to change, so does her thoughts on the subject matter. Don't take anything a woman says too seriously, or attribute it too much importance. **Understand that a woman easily changes her mind, as easily as she changes her mood. DON'T TAKE A WOMAN'S WORDS AS PERMANENT.**

END NOTE

Congratulations on finishing this book. I commend you on investing in yourself to get the practical knowledge that will lead you to success with women. Be willing to review key lessons in this book multiple times to have the lessons really sink in. Go out and conquer!